# Tea Rooms Northwest

### Featuring Tea Rooms,
### Tea Events,
### and Tea Time Recipes

*Sharron and John deMontigny*

J&S Publishing
Corvallis, Oregon USA

The Tea Cup Graphics in this publication
are the property of Pat's Web Graphics.
Other photos are from the private albums of
J&S Publishing and/or were provided by the
Tea Room proprietors.

Cover photo by Renaude
Cover design by Karen Freeman

Also by Sharron and John deMontigny:
Tea Time Journal

**J&S Publishing**
2397 N.W. Kings Blvd. # 148
Corvallis, Oregon 97330 USA
Telephone: 541-753-1502
E-Mail: *demontigny@proaxis.com*
Web Site: *www.teatimeadventures.com*

ISBN # 0-9741814-1-2

Printed in the United States of America
Cascade Printing Company
Corvallis, Oregon USA

J&S Publishing

# TABLE OF CONTENTS

Tea Rooms of Oregon. . . . . . . . . 15

Tea Rooms of Washington . . . . . . 61

Tea Rooms of British Columbia . . . . . 111

Tea Rooms Beyond the Northwest . . . . 131

Tea at Sea . . . . . . . . . . 141

Favorite Recipes
Beverages . . . . . . . . . . 148
Sandwiches, Savories & Soups . . . . 153
Scones, Desserts & Toppings . . . . . 173

Recipe Index . . . . . . . . . . 218

Alphabetical Tea Room Listings
Oregon . . . . . . . . . . . 220
Washington . . . . . . . . . 222
British Columbia . . . . . . . . 224

Tea Room Listings by City
Oregon . . . . . . . . . . . 225
Washington . . . . . . . . . 238
British Columbia . . . . . . . . 231

About Tea Time Adventures . . . . . 234

Did you find a new Tea Room? . . . . . 235

Is Journaling for You? . . . . . . . 236

# About the Cover Photo

*Sharron's family treasures grace the cover of Tea Rooms Northwest. On the table is a 1925 photograph of her mother, O'Day Tynan Robertson. The tablecloth came from Ireland in the 1950's by Sharron's great aunt, Alice Hurley, and the doilies were crocheted by her maternal grandmother, Rose McClory Ritzenthaler. Our grandson Brandon's other grandmother owned the tea set, which was given to Sharron to add to her collection. Tucked away in the picture is a string of pearls, a gift from John to Sharron.*

*Photography by Renaude*

# About the Photographer

*Born in Canada, Renaude learned the love of photography at the elbow of her father, Etienne Grenier, also an accomplished photographer. Renaude migrated to the United States in 1968, and after raising a family, took up the art of photography while living in Los Angeles, California. When she and her family moved to Oregon, she discovered the beauty of the Oregon back roads. Passionate about still life photography, Renaude and her sister regularly roam dusty lanes and byways for inspirational glimpses of scenic barns and pastures.*

# *Promoting the Love of Tea*

As you browse through this book, it will be readily apparent to you which Tea Rooms we enjoyed visiting. It is easy to personalize those pages because writing about them brings back such pleasant memories of our time there. The other Tea Rooms are on our "to do" list, as we continue to visit them for the pure joy it brings us.

Our main interest in publishing this book is to encourage you, the tea lover, to see and visit the many Tea Rooms available to you. Our intent is to share some personal observations, not to either endorse or critique any of them. Tea Rooms Northwest is your resource for finding Tea Rooms, learning specific information about them and a means to get updated information. Remember that prices, hours, locations, etc. change. Check our website *teatimeadventures.com* for regularly updated information. Please feel free to call or email us for information and updates.
Phone: 541-753-1502
e-mail: demontigny@proaxis.com.

When we first began visiting Tea Rooms, we had no idea where this adventure would lead us. Who knew that we would be taking tea tours, publishing a Tea Time Journal, giving presentations and now offering a Tea Room Guide.

We sincerely hope that, with this book in hand, you will now experience more joy in your own Tea Room adventures. We also hope that you will share some of your comments and suggestions with us.

*Sharron*

# About the Authors

John and Sharron reside in Corvallis, Oregon, a college town midway between the mountains and the ocean. Yes, they are avid Beaver fans!

John was born in Quebec, Canada and moved to the states when he was five, settling first on the East Coast. He eventually moved with his family to California where he was raised. After high school, he enlisted in the Air Force where he served for twenty-five years. After retirement in 1991, John went to work for Hewlett Packard, where he is still employed.

Sharron was born and raised in San Francisco and is proud to call herself a "fourth generation San Franciscan." She met John during the summer of 1963 and they were married in 1968, at which time she became a military wife. While raising their three children in California and Oregon, she owned a catering business. Upon their move to Corvallis in 1990, she gave up the business and became a cook for the men of Tau Kappa Epsilon Fraternity, who she calls her "other family."

John and Sharron are also the proud grandparents of four boys and four girls. Fortunately, they all live nearby and are able to visit each other often.

# Disclaimers

We made a sincere effort to find and include **ALL** the tearooms in the Northwest. However, we know that some are missing from this book. If you are a Tea Room owner or if you have a favorite Tea Room that is not in this guide, please let us know. Our website *teatimeadventures.com* will update this guide on a regular basis. Additional Tea Rooms will be listed in the next edition of Tea Rooms Northwest.

***Everything*** is subject to change! The information we have included in this guide was accurate at the time of publication. Tea Rooms may change their ***prices*** (*), days and hours of operation, location and menu offerings. Unfortunately, they also close or discontinue offering tea. We highly recommend that you call ahead before venturing out and remember...some Tea Rooms ***require*** reservations!

(*) The prices quoted in the British Columbia section are in Canadian (CND) funds.

# Acknowledgments

We would like to thank many of the people who helped us to make this book possible, especially Ken and Sharon Foster-Lewis, publishers of *Tea Time in the Northwest*. Without their encouragement we may not have attempted to continue their tradition.

Others who helped us in our search for Tea Rooms, and to whom we are most grateful, are Maureen Wilson, Nancy Goforth and Jill Davis. They took the time to visit Tea Rooms and to share their findings with us. They also encouraged Tea Room owners to contact us.

Sincere thanks also go out to Alicia Jacob, Claudia Byers, Marilyn Bousquet, Pam Darcy and Annette Kessler for their invaluable help with proof-reading our material. It was an arduous job and their efforts are most appreciated. Also, many thanks to Irene Gresick, who shared her publishing expertise.

Last, but certainly not least, we want to acknowledge all of the Tea Room proprietors who returned our questionnaire, took our many phone calls, responded to our e-mails, welcomed us to their Tea Rooms and in every way helped us complete this labor of love. We hope that we are representing you in a manner that pleases and benefits you.

# Dedications

We dedicate this book to out wonderful family: Stephen & Jennifer, Todd & Alicia and Eric & Deanna, in appreciation for all their support and assistance during the writing of this book, and to our grandchildren Brandon, Ashley, Jason, Christian, Jessica, Daphne, Hannah and Marcus, who sacrificed a lot of "grandpa and grandma time" during the last few months. You all bring such joy and happiness to our lives.

We also dedicate this book to "our" mom, Charlotte, whose positive attitude is such an inspiration to us. She has always shown by example that we should never give up on our dreams and aspirations. During the writing of this book, she encouraged us every step of the way.

# Tea with the Grandkids

Ashley

Brandon

Jessica at Julia's
Tea Parlor

Daphne at Joyful
Hearts

Christian at
Ruthie B's

Hanna and her mom
at Joyful Hearts

Jason at Ruthie B's

# The Origin of Tea Time

In the early 1800's in England, dinner was usually served quite late at night. It is said that Anne, the Duchess of Bedford, started having hunger pangs while awaiting the evening meal, which was often served around 9:00 p.m. She requested that a tray of bread and butter, along with a pot of tea, be sent to her room. Soon, along with the tea and bread, dainty pastries with clotted cream and preserves were added. It then became the custom for her to invite some society ladies to join her and "tea time" came into being. Though intended to be an evening snack, it is now what many of us think of as Afternoon Tea, and it is served anywhere between 11:00 a.m. and 4:00 p.m. The other wording for afternoon tea was low tea, as it was served at a low table, much like our modern coffee table.

High Tea was actually the evening meal of the common people, and it was served at the dinner table, or high table. Served around 6:00 p.m., High Tea consisted of trays of meats, cheeses, fish or eggs along with bread & butter, cake and tea. Side dishes were often added to the meal. Today, many Tea Rooms serve a Ploughman's Plate, which is much the same meal.

It seems that one was more suited to women and the other to men. One was a diversion and the other a meal for the working man!

## Brewing Tips

Always start with cold water.
Heat your teapot with warm water (hot could
crack you pot).
Add one teaspoon of tea leaves per cup
(a heaping teaspoon for iced).
Do not over-boil the water.

## Black Teas

Bring water to a rolling boil and remove from
heat. Add tea and steep for 5 minutes. If you like
a stronger, pungent cup of tea, add a bit more
tea. Steeping longer than 5 minutes will produce
a bitter tea.

## Green and Pouchong Teas

Bring water to a pre-boil and remove from heat.
Add tea and steep 3 minutes. Quality green teas
can be steeped more than once.

## Oolong and White Teas

Bring water to a pre-boil. Add tea and steep 4-6
minutes. Oolongs can vary in steeping time so
taste to test. They can be re-steeped several
times.

## Tisanes (Herbals)

Bring water to a rolling boil. Add herbs, one
heaping teaspoon per cup (for iced herbals, add
one tablespoon). Steep 5-9 minutes. Herbs will
not get bitter if left longer.

When your day seems topsy-turvy
And as stormy as can be,
There's nothing quite as tranquil
As a nice hot cup of tea.

While you savor this ambrosia
Your problems fade away,
It's warmth will bring you comfort
And brighten up your day.

So take a private moment,
There's a calmness, as you'll see
All because you briefly stopped
To sip a cup of tea.

Courtesy of Bigelow Tea website

# Welcome

# to

# Oregon

# A La Fontaine Tea Room
## and Day Spa
*1708 Springhill Dr. N.W.*
*Albany, Oregon 97321*
*541-928-0747 / 800-531-4306*
*l.bardell@juno.com / www.alafontaine.com*

*From I-5, follow signs for downtown Albany, then for Hwy 20 / Corvallis.*
*Cross the bridge, take a right and go approximately 1 mile (between Quarry*
*and Ferguson Sts). Just past Quarry watch for the Nebergal intersection.*

More than a tea room, A La Fontaine offers a recipe for relaxation along
with afternoon tea selections. Located in a turn of the century home, tea
may be taken in the Old World Garden or in the Grand Manor Tea Room.
During the warm season, the garden veranda patio is an added venue.

Linda and Andrew offer a spa menu that features everything from mas-
sages and facials to mineral soaks and a quiet room. There are three spa
packages available for $99.00 to $249.00 as well as many ala carte options.
A light tea of fruit, cheese and crackers for $10.00 or a wrap sandwich and
tea for $15.00 may be added to any of the above spa choices.

The tea menu consists of five options ranging from the Tea Break, which
consists of tea and scones with jam, lemon curd and crème fraiche for $6.99
to the Full Afternoon Tea of scones, crème fraiche, lemon curd, fruit, a
variety of tea sandwiches, cheese & crackers with quiche and dessert for
$19.99. Other choices are the Tea Brunch, Tea Lunch and Tea Escape which
range in price from $9.99 to $15.99. All teas include scones or crumpets and
lemon curd, crème fraiche and tea. The proprietors will work with food
allergies and special diets and will offer whole foods/organic whenever
possible.

Special theme teas such as International, Holiday, Bridal, etc. may be
arranged. Doll collectors may want to gather for tea since another business,
L.B. Designs, a doll sculpting studio and school, is located on the premises.

MC/V/AE/DC/DIS/Checks    Wheelchair Accessible    Parking Lot

*Open Tues-Sat 10-8 by reservation only. Tea is served 11-1 and 3-5. Reser-*
*vations required 1 week in advance. There is a non refundable deposit if*
*cancelled in less that 24 hours. Groups of 4-15 inside / unlimited outside.*

*Proprietor's*
*Autograph*_____*Date*_____

# *Afternoon Delight*
## *Tea Room & Gifts*
*831 S.E. Cass Street*
*Roseburg, Oregon 97470*
*541-677-9010*

*From I-5, take exit 125 and go East. At Rose Street turn right. Go one block to Cass Street and turn left. The tea room is on the right*

This tea room may become a sentimental favorite since Roseburg was our home for ten years and John once had an office in this building. How things change! Sharon has done a wonderful job of transforming this space into a charming "garden themed" tea room, surrounded by lavender walls, that offers everything we are looking for when seeking out that afternoon "delight". There are floral tablecloths, comfortable chairs, lace curtained windows and an eclectic mix of bone china and dishes.

As for the tea offerings, there are five to choose from starting with a Sandwich or Dessert Tea for $4.95 to the High Tea for $12.95. High Tea includes 2 scones, 5 tea sandwiches and savories, meat pastry, 5 desserts and a pot of Longbottom Tea. Soup of the day is also available for $2.95 or it may be substituted for the chicken pastry on High Tea. Special teas are

offered seasonally and the tea room may be reserved after hours for showers, birthdays, anniversaries, business meetings, etc. After enjoying your respite from reality, take time to browse through the "delightful" gift area.

Checks or Cash          Wheelchair Accessible          Lot and Street Parking

*Hours of operation are Tuesday through Saturday from 11-4. One day advance reservations are required for groups of 5 or more. There is a $1.50 split plate charge.*

*Proprietor's*
*Autograph*_____*Date*_____

17

# *Afternoon Tea by Stephanie*

*508 S.E. 9th Avenue*
*Canby, Oregon 97013*
*503-266-7612*
*stephtea@juno.com*

*Owner Stephanie Allen is an instructor for tea and etiquette. Her presentations are at various locations in the Northwest.*

Stephanie does presentations for women , "For the Love of Teacups" and "Silver, Enriching Our Lives" as well as workshops for youth, which are age specific. They include Etiquette for Youth for 8-12 year olds, which ends with a tea party. The Dining With Style for Teens includes a three course dinner to practice their new skills. For the 4-7 year olds, there are Imaginary Tea Parties complete with tea sets, hats and gloves. These classes are taught at various locations including the Historic Deepwood Estate in Salem and Carnegie Center in Oregon City. Special dietary needs can be accommodated with advance notice.

Stephanie retails Simpson and Vale teas, along with her special tea accessories, at Deepwood Estate in Salem and Carnegie Center.

She is making plans to offer traditional teas in the near future.

MC/V/and Checks Accepted

*For dates and times of workshops, or to schedule your own, contact Stephanie directly.*

*Proprietor's*
*Autograph*_____ *Date*_____

# *Albertina's*

## *Albertina Kerr Center*

*424 NE 22nd Avenue*
*Portland, Oregon 97232*
*503-231-3909 / 503-231-0216*
*www.albertinakerr.org*

*They are located near Lloyd Center and Oregon Convention Center close to the intersection of Sandy Blvd. and 20th.*

The house that has become The Shops at Albertina Kerr has a long and interesting history. Located on land that was donated by Alexander Kerr, founder of the Kerr Jar Manufacturing Co., it became a care center for children in 1921. The nursery closed in 1967 then re-opened in 1981 as the Old Kerr Nursery, housing the present volunteer-staffed Shops at Albertina Kerr. Some of the current programs which benefit from the shops include foster care for children with special needs, early intervention programs, psychiatric residential services, group home and supportive living services for people with developmental disabilities and more. The businesses which comprise The Shops at Albertina Kerr include a gift shop, antiques shop, thrift shop and Albertina's, which offers luncheons and catering.

Though primarily a luncheon restaurant, Albertina's is described as having a "tea room" atmosphere. Once a year that atmosphere becomes a reality when a Valentines Tea is offered on a Saturday afternoon in February. A sample menu consists of ribbon tea sandwiches, chive and egg pinwheels, chicken almond fingers, lemon tartlets, fudge party bars, chocolate-dipped strawberries, sugared grapes and tea or coffee. Sherry and wine may be purchased at an additional cost.

This would be a wonderful opportunity to take tea in a very special setting while helping out this very worthwhile organization. Mark your calendar now so you don't forget about this very special event!

The property is available to rent for special events and there is an in-house caterer.

MC/V/Checks          Wheelchair Accessible          Lot and Street Parking

*Luncheon seatings are at 11:30 and 1:00 Monday through Friday.*
*Reservations are required. They offer an annual Valentines Tea.*

*Proprietor's*
*Autograph_____Date_____*

# Althea's Tea Room

*184 S.E. Oak Street*
*Dallas, OR 97338*
*503-831-4777*
*Pme16@msn.com*

*Heading west from Salem on Hwy 22, follow signs to Dallas. Once in Dallas, at the second signal keep to the left onto Main Street. Continue to Oak St. and turn left. The tea room is on the left hand side at the end of the block.*

How pleased we were to find that another tea room had opened so close to home. It's a very pleasant drive from Corvallis to Dallas and I think we will be taking that route fairly often!

Patricia, who opened her business in October of 2003, named it in honor of her mother and she is assisted by her friendly and capable daughter Frances. Situated in an older building in the downtown area, Althea's is a welcoming and warm place to sit and sip. The two rooms, one a pale yellow and the other a soft green, have large lace covered windows, tables decked out in pink rose patterned cloths with coordinating napkins, and white "doilies" at each place setting. Customers select their cup and saucer from the antique cabinet which is tucked in the corner. The tea pots are wrapped in pretty cozies and the tea sets are presented on tiered servers.

On our recent visit, we decided to have Dena's Tea. It consisted of tea sandwiches, fresh fruit, assorted sweets and a delicious scone with clotted cream, lemon curd and strawberry jam for $8.95. The other two tea sets are Hanna's Tea, which is scones and tea for $4.00 and Bethany's Tea, which is tea sandwiches, cheese selection, seasonal fruit, savories, assorted sweets, scones with all the trimmings and a pot of tea for $12.95.

Lunch items are also available and may include soup or quiche of the day, sandwiches, or Fran's Pear Salad. Specialty desserts are featured as well as coffee, lemonade and iced tea. Themed teas are planned for the future, as are Holiday events.

MC/V/Checks     Wheelchair Accessible     Free Street Parking

*The tea room is open from 10-5, Tues. through Sat. Lunch is served from 11-2. Tea is available from 11-4. Tea reservations are required 24 hours in advance for more that 4 people and are recommended for all others. Tea and scones are served all day.*

*Proprietor's*
*Autograph_____Date_____*

# Ashland Springs Hotel

212 East Main Street
Ashland, Oregon 97520
541-488-1701
www.ashlandspringshotel.com

*Northbound I-5, take exit 11 onto Hwy 99. Go 5 mi. to down-town. Turn left on 1ˢᵗ. Southbound take exit 19 go rt. to 1ˢᵗ light, left at hwy 99. Go 2 mi. The hotel is at 1ˢᵗ and E Main St.*

The 1925 Ashland Springs Hotel, which is a Historic Landmark, offers a Sunday afternoon tea on the mezzanine, overlooking the beautifully appointed lobby. The tables are covered with floor length linen cloths and are set with crisp napkins, silver accessories and fine china. Grand windows give warmth to the room, while fresh flowers and numerous palm trees add to the feeling that you are welcome here.

Afternoon tea consists of a pot of tea, assorted tea sandwiches, scones with strawberry preserves, lemon curd and Devonshire Cream, house-smoked salmon, Oregon cheeses and toast points, chocolate dipped fruits and fresh grapes, dessert delicacies, and raspberry cordial, dry sherry or cranberry fizz. Tiered servers adorn the tables and the cost per person is $23.00.

Vegetarian Available upon Request     Wheelchair Accessible
MC/V/AE/DC/DIS/JCB/Checks and Room charge Accepted

*Tea is served on Sundays from 3-5pm. Reservations are highly recommended though walk-in's are welcome. Large groups and private parties can be accommodated with prior reservation.*

*Proprietor's
Autograph_____ Date_____*

# Blue Angel Heavenly Delectables

10500 S.E. 26th # A33
Milwaukie, Oregon 97222
503-975-9744
blueangelbake@yahoo.com

*Teas are on location and place is to be determined at time of booking.*

Elise Hamilton offers private teas only, either at your location of choice or at the historic Broetje House in Milwaukie. Built in 1889, the home offers the perfect ambiance for your special tea. The banquet room can seat up to 150 people and is available for weddings, retirements, birthdays and other events as well.

Blue Angel Custom Bakery uses only the freshest, highest quality, natural ingredients to prepare your unique menu. Many of the recipes are one of a kind and each menu is made to order. The tea menu offers tea and scones for $8.00 up to a High Tea package for $22.00. All teas include scones and there is a list of 74 to choose from. Dessert is included in High Tea only but may be added to the other teas at a cost of $1.50-$3.50 per person. Tea Zone is the house tea and coffee is available upon request.

Some of the tea choices include entrée soup or salad and the selection is extensive. Elise encourages you to make your event unique by offering some basic packages to which you may add selected items. All packages include a choice of Premium Exotic Tea.

Specialty items are a tart, pastries and an old family recipe for potato cheese enchiritos. As for dessert...just reading the list was a pleasure! There are bars, tortes, tarts, crisps, cakes, cookies, breads and muffins. Where to begin?

MC/V/Checks          Wheelchair Accessible          Large Parking Lot

*Tea is by reservation only. A 50% nonrefundable deposit is required at time of booking. Call for further information.*

*Proprietor's*
*Autograph*_____*Date*_____

# Butteville General Store

*10767 Butte Street. NE*
*Aurora, Oregon 97002*
*503-678-1605*
*forrestgalley@msn.com / www.buttevillegeneralstore.com*

*From I-5, take exit 282B (Charbonneau) and drive west on Butteville Road*
*for approximately 5 miles. The road follows the Willamette River.*

It is so special to see historic sites starting to offer tea on their premises. The 1863 Butteville Store, with it's French Prairie design, is just such an example of this trend. Though Barbara and Rob offer other items for sale, this venture into tea is the one I am so excited about.

Afternoon Tea, which is $12.00 per person, offers a pot of tea, scones, Marionberry jam, Devon Cream, tea sandwiches and a variety of desserts. You may choose a pot of tea and scones for $6.00. Tea is served in the rustic setting of the general store, surrounded by antiques and other memorabilia.

Besides tea, deli items are available whenever they are open and they include soup, sandwiches and salads, as well as other beverages and desserts. Friday night is Pizza night and Candlelit Heritage Dinners are presented periodically.

After a leisurely tea, take a little extra time to look about the store at the gift items available. They include items that you would find in a historical general store...candles, soaps, etc. The Forrest Gallery offers paintings, ceramics, hand woven baskets, and blown glass, plus more local artists work.

The store is part of Champoeg State Heritage Area and is another Oregon treasure. Take time to admire and appreciate her!

MC/V      Wheelchair Accessible      Free Street and Lot Parking

*Hours are seasonal. They are open daily in the Summer and on Wednesday*
*through Sunday in the Fall. Tea time is 1-4 in the Fall, Winter and Spring on*
*Wed, Thurs, Fri and Sun. Reservations required. Call for specifics.*

*Proprietor's*
*Autograph_____Date_____*

# The Campbell House Inn

## B & B and Tea Room

252 Pearl Street
Eugene, Oregon 97401
541-343-1119 / www.campbellhouse.com

*From I-5, take exit 194B onto I-105 then take the Coburg/Downtown exit. Stay left and follow City Center/Mall signs. Cross river, turn right at 2nd exit (Downtown/Hult Center-Hwy 126). Make an immediate right at the signal onto High Street. Turn left on 5th Ave then turn right on to Pearl St. You will see the Inn on the left side of the street. Pull into the drive at the sign and enter the large parking lot.*

This lovely bed and breakfast is located at the foot of Skinners Butte, within walking distance to 5th Street Market. An expansive yellow "Victorian House", you are immediately impressed by it from the outside, but more delights await you upon entering. Every room is beautifully appointed with antique furnishings and complementary accessories. There are over 30 guest rooms and each, with its distinctive name, is decorated uniquely and creatively. When you attend one of the special teas hosted by Campbell House, the owners welcome you to view the guest rooms that are not occupied. That is a special treat worth taking advantage of! The tour allows you to linger a little longer after tea, before heading back to reality.

Teas are offered twice a year, so remember to make reservations well in advance and mark your calendar. Afternoon tea begins with a delicious frozen mousse, which is served individually plated, followed by scones with jam and cream. The last two courses are served together on a tiered server and consist of three types of sandwiches; chicken/hazelnut, cucumber/dill and pineapple/ham. The assorted desserts vary but may be apricot truffles, cream puffs, fruitcake, fruit and nut bread or a chocolate truffle. Tea is poured and additional sandwiches are offered. The cost of the tea is $21.00 per person and the Christmas tea includes carolers for entertainment. Special children's teas are offered at noon during the year, and they have special themes and programs at a cost of $18.00 per child.

There are two sittings per day at 12:30 and 3:00. They both fill up quickly so reserve early. Don't risk missing out, since these wonderful teas only come around twice a year!

MC/V/Dis/AE/Diners/Checks
Wheelchair Accessible          Lot Parking          Lot Parking

*Teas are offered on Mother's Day weekend. Christmas Tea's are offered on numerous weekends during December. Reservations required. Call for further information regarding groups. (see WEB page)*

Proprietor's
Autograph_____Date_____

# Columbia Gorge Hotel

*4000 Westcliff Drive*
*Hood River, Oregon 97031-9970*
*541-386-5566 / 800-345-1921*
*www.ColumbiaGorgeHotel.com*

*Take I-84 to Exit 62 and follow the signs. The Hotel is right there.*

How nice it is to see another fine hotel offering afternoon tea. Time was, when all the big resort and city hotels offered tea but unfortunately many have ceased that tradition. Thank you, Boyd and Halla for bringing it to the Gorge. This beautiful hotel, built in 1921, is referred to as a "Romantic Jazz-Age Hotel" and it is a national landmark. After your relaxing tea time, spend a little time walking around the hotel and taking in all the beauty she has to offer, both inside and out.

Tea is served in the beautiful dining room overlooking the grounds of the hotel. White linens, elegant china, sparkling crystal and fresh flowers grace the table, and tiered silver servers provide the finishing touch. The set consists of assorted Columbia Gorge Hotel specialty sandwiches, scrumptious Scones with Crème Royale and jam, seasonal fresh fruit, gourmet chocolate dipped strawberries, assorted petit fours, delectable strawberry shortcake parfait and a pot of delightful tea . The cost is $21.95 per person. Special theme teas will be provided on request and changes in the menu may be made at the customers request.

I have heard from a "reliable source" that this is a trip worth making, though I would like to add a weekend stay at this fabulous hotel! I have heard that their breakfast and dinner offerings are also wonderful!

MC/V/AE/DIS/Checks    Wheelchair Accessible    Lot Parking

*High tea is served on Sundays from 1-4. Reservations are not required but are recommended. Tea is served to groups anytime by reservation.*

*Proprietor's*
*Autograph*_____*Date*_____

# Deepwood Estate

*1116 Mission Street S.E.*
*Salem, Oregon 97302*
*503-363-1825*
*deepwood@open.org*

*From I-5 take the Mission Street exit. Head west on Mission. Turn left on 12th. The house is on the corner of Mission and 12th. The parking lot is on the corner of 12th and Lee.*

Deepwood Estate, which is owned by the city of Salem, is a beautifully restored 1894 Queen Ann style home. It is surrounded by a formal English garden where many afternoon tea events are held. The first tea was presented in 1998 for a volunteer's daughter and the rest, as they say, is history. The tea hostess, Janice Palmquist, studied the Victorian and English traditions and has developed menus which incorporate many period recipes. Attention to detail is evident at every tea she oversees, from the collection of teacups and saucers to the vintage linens which grace the tables. All of the afternoon teas are four courses and include seasonal fruit, cream scones, assorted finger sandwiches and miniature tea desserts. The cost of the tea is $22.00 prepaid. Janice is planning to offer 5 course themed teas in the near future. There are also several special teas during the year including a Christmas Victorian Tea, Autumn Tea and Valentines Tea as well as a Summer Garden Tea, a Fall Knitting Tea and others. Special dietary needs can be accommodated with advance request.

MC/V/DIS/Checks        Gift Shop        Not Wheelchair Accessible

*Proprietor's*
*Autograph*_____*Date*_____

# Eve's Garden Café & Tea Room

15090 Highway 238
Applegate, OR 97530
541-846-9019
info@edensgatefarms.com

*From I-5, take exit 58 at Grants Pass and proceed to intersection for Williams Hwy/Hwy 238. Take that highway toward Murphy and continue to the town of Applegate. From I-5 in Medford, take exit 30 and head west on Hwy. 238 through the town of Jacksonville. Continue another 15 miles to the town of Applegate. They relocated to downtown Applegate.*

Eve's Garden Café, which is owned by Cathy and Paula, opened in 2002 and is located at Eden's Gate Farms in historic Applegate. The quaint tea room is located n a 1890's cottage and boasts a whimsical décor complete with painted clouds on the ceiling and ivy on the floor. The windows are decorated with antique hankie valances, and the tables are covered with antique cloths. Outside seating is offered in the summer in their beautiful rose and flower gardens. What better setting for dress up tea parties featuring Victorian hats, vintage attire, gloves and boas? Cathy and Paula call their parties, "a great escape for a few hours of fun".

High Tea, which is by reservation only, would be the perfect event for an anniversary, shower, retirement, business luncheon, or any other special occasion. Actually, no reason is needed. A chance to get away is reason enough! At a cost of $10.00 for children and $16.00 for adults, the tea offers scones with Devonshire cream and lemon curd, soup or salad, finger sandwiches and quiche, sorbet or fruit, an assortment of desserts and a selection of teas to choose from for your bottomless pot

Besides high tea, breakfast item such as French toast made with Hazelnut bread and a croissant sandwich are offered. Lunch specialties include quiche, salads, sandwiches and soups. You might be tempted to try Eatin' From the Garden, a double-decker vegetarian sandwich or Gobble Till You Wobble, the cook's favorite turkey sandwich.

Catering is available for groups up to 25 during the winter and for up to 125 in the summer. The tea room shares space with a gift shop so plan to stay awhile! What ever you are looking for, tea for two or tea for a crowd, this little bit of heaven is the perfect location for a brief respite.

MC/V/DEB          Wheelchair Accessible          Parking Lot

*Open Wed-Fri 8-3, Sat and Sun 9-3. High tea is served any time with 24 hour reservation notice. Your credit card will be charged if you fail to show at the appointed time. A gratuity added for groups of 5 or more. Baked goods, tea and lunch are available at all times.*

Proprietor's
Autograph_____Date_____

# Flinn's Tea Room

222 First Avenue West
Albany, Oregon 97321
541-791-5347

*From I-5, take the Albany exit. Follow the signs to Hwy 20 (Corvallis/
Albany City Center). Turn left on 1st Ave. and go 1 1/2 blocks. The Flinn
Building is on the left hand side and the tea room is just inside the red doors.*

Flinn's Tea Room is located in the Historic Flinn Block, which was built
in 1887 to house Albany's first bank, the First National Bank, by founder
and president Judge Flinn. The 5000 square foot second floor was occupied
mostly by the prominent attorneys in town. The bank moved to a new location in 1909 and by the 30's, the upper floors were mostly converted     apart-
ments. In 1975 the main floor was converted into Albany's first     shopping
mall, Fannie Flinn's Custom House. Today the building houses the tea room,
Flinn's Café and Aromatique on the first floor and Flinn's Living History
Theater on the second floor.

Flinn's is offering tea again under the new owner, Shannon, and it is a
completely different kind of tea than was offered there in the past.  The ambiance is Victorian Garden style and the choices numerous. You may now
select the style of tea and menu that you want and the prices range from
$7.50 to $21.00. The teas include various finger sandwiches, breads, scones,
desserts, specialty drinks and a large tea selection. High Tea also includes an
entrée. If you prefer, there is a lunch menu to select from as well. Coffee is
available on request.

There is a small gift shop which sells tea related items such as clotted
cream, lemon curd and varieties of teas. Outside catering is available and
groups are welcome.

MC/V/AE/DIS/Checks     Wheelchair Accessible     Free Street Parking

*Teas are by reservation and are available Monday through Saturday 11-9.
Reservations are required at least 24 hours in advance as is confirmation
number.*

*Proprietor's
Autograph*_____*Date*_____

# The Gordon House at the Oregon Gardens

*P.O. Box 155*
*Silverton, Oregon 97381*
*503-874-6006 / 877-674-2733 ext. 6006*
*gordonhouse@oregongardens.org*

*The house is located at the Oregon Gardens property,*
*which is 15 miles east of Salem on Silverton Road.*

We have had the pleasure of visiting both the gardens and the Gordon House in Silverton. Having grown up hearing about Frank Lloyd Wright, it was especially memorable to be able to visit the only house in Oregon that was designed by him. It is also his only building open to the public in the Northwest. How sad it would have been, had the house been destroyed!

I met Molly, the coordinator, at a tea class we took together. Her interest in tea, and her desire to present teas which will benefit the Gordon House, are note worthy.

Teas are presented during specific months of the year and reservations need to be made from two months to two days in advance, as available. The setting is a home that features Frank Lloyd Wright's "economic design for middle-class American families". It provides the tea-goes a unique and artistic setting for tea and lunch. How special it is for us, to be able to actually sit down and relax as a guest of the Gordon House!

The tea venue changes from tea to tea and some of the menus follow a particular theme. An example would be the Russian Tea; Russian Caravan black tea, Georgia black tea, Honey Lemon Ginseng Herb tea, cream scones with fig jam and lime curd, salmon quiche with medium Cheddar cheese, and finger sandwiches of herbed cream cheese with cucumber, open-face Albacore tuna and smoked turkey and chutney roll-ups. A salad of mixed organic greens with Imperial Russian Vinaigrette dressing and Anastasia cake complete the meal, which costs $35.00 per person. Sounds wonderful!

The best part about taking tea at the Gardens is that the proceeds continue the restoration and preservation of the house.

MC/V/AE/DIS/Checks    Wheelchair Accessible    Free Parking
Total seating capacity is 25-40 people and groups are welcome.

*The house is open daily, November 1 through February, 10-3 and March*
*through October, 10-5. Teas are scheduled for November through*
*February, every Sat. from 12-2, one seating per day. By reservation only.*

*Proprietor's*
*Autograph_____Date_____*

# The Heathman Restaurant

*1001 S.W. Broadway*
*Portland, Oregon 97205*
*503-790-7752*

*Located in the Heathman Hotel at the corner of Broadway and Salmon in downtown Portland.*

The Heathman is an elegant Old World hotel which offers tea in the elegant lobby amid crystal chandeliers, wood paneling and eucalyptus. A working fireplace adds to the charm of this historic tea room.

The afternoon tea, which is $18.00 per person, includes sandwiches, savories, congolais and cookies, cake, scone, lemon tartlet and a pot of tea. The Peter Rabbit Tea for "little sippers" consists of a sandwich, cheese blocks, congolais and cookies, fruit, goldfish crackers, teddy grahams and hot chocolate for $8.95. Sparkling and Sweets by the glass are also available. The house tea is Fonte Coffee & Tea Co. out of Seattle, Washington and there is a generous selection of regular and decaffeinated teas. Coffee is available upon request as is a full lunch menu.

The lobby is wheelchair accessible.
MC/V/DIS/CB/AE and Checks Accepted

*Tea is served 7 days a week from November to January and on weekends only February to October from 12-4pm. Reservations are required with cancellation call requested.*

*Proprietor's*
*Autograph*_____*Date*_____

30

# In Good Taste

*231 N.W. 11ᵗʰ Avenue*
*Portland, Oregon 97209*
*503 248 2015*
*bdawson@igtoregon.com / www.ingoodtastestore.com*

*From I-5 No., take 405 exit (towards Beaverton) then Everett St. exit. Turn*
*left on Everett and proceed to 11th St. From So on I-5, take 405 (towards*
*City Center). Take Everett St. exit and go to 11ᵗʰ. You're there!*

This afternoon tea opportunity was a real find and we would never have found it on our own. Thanks, Jill!! It is situated in the back of a bustling retail business which offers every kind of kitchen equipment you could ask for, delicious Bistro faire, wine tasting, outside catering and cooking classes. Luckily, Barbara Dawson hails from England and felt a need to add tea time to the list of offerings at In Good Taste.

Tea the beverage is offered every day until 4:00 but afternoon tea, as we have come to know it, is only offered from 2-4 by reservation. A group of us ventured in one sunny afternoon and were seated by the window at small tables with white linens and dishes and a single red rose. We had the only flowers! Our tea, from the Tea Zone, was served quickly in individual pots with scrumptious scones and individual servers of cream, jam and clotted cream. The remainder of the offerings, which were delivered on tiered servers, consisted of sandwiches and desserts. Additional sandwiches and desserts were offered and accepted! The cost of the tea was $14.95 and included very friendly service along with delicious food.

MC/V/AE/DC/DIS/JCB
There is metered parking as well as a parking lot.

*Retail store: Mon-Sat. 10-6 and Sun. 10-5. Bistro: Breakfast - Mon-Fri.*
*8-11, Lunch - Mon-Fri. 11-3, Weekends - 8-3. Tea is served daily until 4pm.*
*Afternoon tea 2-4pm by reservation.*

*Proprietor's*
*Autograph_____Date_____*

# Joyful Hearts Tea Room

## and Gift Shop

134 N.W. 4th Street
Corvallis, Oregon 97330
541-738-1100
joyheartstearoom@yahoo.com / www.joyfulhearts.org

*From Hwy 34, come into town and turn left at 4th Street. Get into the right lane and go 2+ blocks. The tea room is on the right hand side of the street.*

Joyful Hearts is a most welcome addition to downtown Corvallis, giving shoppers the opportunity to take a break in a wonderful and relaxing atmosphere. The first thing you notice upon entering Joyful Hearts is the delightful fragrance. Then, almost immediately, you hear the sound of a miniature waterfall and classical music in the background. The soft yellow and green walls compliment the Cottage Garden style and the splashes of pink add to the charming ambiance. The gift shop greets you and gives you a place to linger while waiting to take tea. You will find a generous selection of tea accoutrements, garden themed items, specialty foods and gifts, as well as a large variety of Harney and Son's bulk teas.

Dawn offers an assortment of items to tempt your palate, the most recent additions being soup and a warm oatmeal spice cake. Everything is made fresh on the premises and the menu changes weekly. Prices range from the Scottish Tea which is tea and two scones for $5.25 to a full Afternoon Tea for $13.95 which offers fruit medley, cup of soup, three finger sandwiches, two savories, a cheese wedge, one scone with cream, jam and marmalade, three desserts and candied nuts *or* their signature spicy cake. Other tea sets are available for $7.25 to $10.95 and all include a pot of tea for one. The Mad Hatter's tea for children is available for $2.95 to $4.95.

MC/V/AE/DC/DIS     Wheelchair Accessible     Street Parking

*The shop is open from 10:00 to 5:00 Tuesday through Saturday. Tea is served from 10:00 to 4:00. Groups are welcome. Reservations are required for groups of 8 or more.*

Proprietor's
Autograph_____Date_____

# Julia's Tea Parlor

2280 Wallace Road N.W.
Salem, Oregon 97304
503-378-7060 / 888-224-1821
juliastea@comcast.net

*Take I-5 to Hwy 22 exit. Proceed through town, and cross the Marion Street
Bridge. Stay to the right. Take the West Salem / Dayton exit (Wallace Rd.).
Go right-proceed approximately 1 1/2 miles. The tea room is on the right.*

If you are a history buff and incurable romantic, Julia's will give you a
taste of both. This 150 year old farmhouse on the outskirts of Salem has a
wonderful story to tell. Ed will share the history of the house and how it got
its name, while you sip tea and enjoy the attractive sandwiches and delicious
scones prepared by his wife, Kathleen. Choosing your tea is a treat in itself,
because you sniff the many small apothecary jars until you find just the right
one. Savor your tea, listen to the tale of Julia's humble beginnings, and relax
in the comfort of this charming tearoom. Perhaps you will be there on a cool
day and can sit before the huge stone fireplace with its massive mantle. Or
maybe it will be nice enough to take tea in the garden. Either way, atmosphere abounds at Julia's. And, if you have forgotten your hat, there are numerous ones resting on the backs of the chairs in the tearoom as well as
some proper wraps should you get chilly.

The tea itself is a work of art, with seasonal flowers and rose petals scattered on the tiered servers. Five tea choices are available: a scone and tea for
$5.95, Cream Tea which adds fruit to the above for $7.95. The Lighter Fare
of tea, scone, tea sandwiches and fruit garnish for $9.95. The Light After-
noon Tea which consists of a scone, fresh fruit, 4 tea sandwiches and a selection of decadent afternoon desserts for $14.95 and finally, The Full After-
noon Tea which adds a house quiche of the day to the afternoon tea for
$17.95. All include a pot of tea, Devonshire cream and lemon curd. For chil-
dren 10 and under, Kathleen prepares a Wee Peoples Tea of hot cocoa or tea,
peanut butter & jelly and cheese tea sandwiches, fruit and dessert for $6.95.
Whatever your choice, all are delicious and attractive offerings!

While there, browse through the many gift items available for purchase
in the tea room as well as the gift shop located in the entry area.

MC/V/AE/Checks          Not Wheelchair Accessible          Lot Parking

*Tea room hours are Tuesday through Saturday 10-4. Reservations are
requested 24 hours in advance and groups are welcome.*

*Proprietor's
Autograph_____Date_____*

# Kashin Tei Tea House

*611 S.W. Kingston Avenue*
*Portland, Oregon 97201*
*503-223-9233*
*www.japanesegarden,com*

*Located west of the Rose Gardens and Tennis courts in Washington Park.*
*Call the Japanese Garden Society at 503-223-4070 for specific directions.*

This authentic 4 1/2 mat tea room from Japan, whose name translates to Flower Heart Hut, is owned and operated by the Japanese Garden Society of Oregon. The tea presentation may be viewed by the public May through September, on the 3rd Saturday of the month from 1:00 to 2:00. This is during the Japanese Garden operating hours.

Private party experiences for 5-10 guests are available for a fee of $100.00 and up. Guests will be served a Japanese tea sweet and bowl of Matcha, which is a powdered green tea.

To arrange a private experience of Chanoya (tea of water) or Chado (path of tea), call the Japanese Tea Society and they will provide the names and phone numbers of certified teachers.

The Japanese Garden has a gift shop for your enjoyment.

Not Wheelchair Accessible          Parking lot and on street parking.

*Call the Japanese Garden Society for specific information.*

*Proprietor's*
*Autograph*_____*Date*_____

# KJ's Tea House

*337 Second Avenue S.W.*
*Albany, Oregon 97321*
*541-967-1829 / fax 541-967-0193*

*From I-5, take exit 234B and follow the signs to City Center onto Lyons*
*Street. Turn left on 1st St, go 3 blocks to Ferry and turn left. Go one block to*
*2nd and turn left again. The tea room is on the left side of the street, across*
*from Two Rivers market.*

This "bistro style' restaurant which doubles as a tea room was a real find! Located in the historic district of Albany, Karen and Jessie bring fun to dining with their whimsical décor, flying chefs on the wall and hat collection in the "powder room".

My first visit was with a group of 18, and Karen set a single row of white linen topped tables down the center of the room to accommodate us. The tables were set with eclectic tea cups and saucers, and the tea was served promptly when we were all seated. Thick clotted cream and lemon curd were pre-set and the scones on which to spread them followed right behind the tea. Grape clusters and strawberry fans surrounded the scones making for a very attractive presentation. Though we were never rushed, sandwiches and savories followed the scones, and the dessert platters finished off the offerings. There were four types of sandwiches, all quite tasty, and four different desserts. The cost of the afternoon "Tea and Treats" is $10.50 and bottomless pots of tea are included. Off - site teas are offered and special theme teas may be arranged. A special tea is offered during the Historical Home Tours that Albany is noted for.

When not presenting teas and running a very successful catering business, Karen arranges cooking classes for the public. Ethnic cooking, as well as kids cuisine and chocolate confections, are a sampling of the types of classes offered. To find out more about the classes, call or fax Karen.

MC/V/AE/Checks          Wheelchair Accessible          Street and Lot Parking

*Tea served on Saturdays at 11:00, 12:30 and 2:00. Reservations are*
*required 24 hours in advance. The cancellation policy is also 24 hours in*
*advance. Groups are welcome and if there are 6 or more, special times may*
*be arranged.*

*Proprietor's*
*Autograph_____Date_____*

# La Tea Da Tea Room

904 Main Avenue
Tillamook, Oregon 977140
503-842-5447
tea@lateada-tearoom/ www.lateada-tearoom

*They are located on Hwy. 101 South, which is a one-way street heading south, at the corner of Main and 9th Street.*

It has never failed that when we head north to Tillamook, the rain accompanies us. No matter!! We can step inside La Tea Da and forget all about what is going on outside. The beautiful tea room, opened in 2001 by Terry and Suzanne, just says welcome, come in and relax. It boasts lavender and pale yellow décor, lovely floral arrangements, an eclectic collection of antique furnishings, and just enough lace to please this sentimental Irish lass. If seating is not available right away, you can take advantage of the wait by looking through the wonderful gift shop which features hand-painted teapots and teacups, silver serving pieces, English bone china and imported jams, jellies and teas– the essential ingredients for taking tea at home. Unique picture frames, tassels, swags, Tiffany-style lamps, candles and bath products are available as is complimentary gift wrapping.

Once seated in the tea room, sit back and take in the surroundings while you make your choice from the numerous tea sets. One may choose the Queen Mum's tea which offers something sweet and a pot tea or the Cuppa Tea with it's three scones and pot of tea, each of which is $6.95. The Villagers Tea consists of sorbet, soup, scones *or* tea sandwiches and a pot of tea for $8.95 and the Governors Tea, preferred by gentlemen, consists of sorbet, a selection of sandwiches and savories, scones, a little sweet and a pot of tea for $11.95. The tea that receives raves is the La Tea Da High Tea! It is served on a lovely three tiered server which is laden with tea sandwiches, savories, sweet and Tillamook cheese scones served with jam, lemon curd & Devonshire cream and a selection of dainty and ever-so-tasty desserts, all for $14.95. For the children thee is a Scamp's tea with bite-sized sandwiches and sweets, sorbet and a whimsical tot's pot of tea for $5.95. There is something for everyone and every morsel is delicious! Special events teas are offered and there is a wonderful private room for groups.

MC/V/Checks          Wheelchair Accessible          Free Street Parking

*The shop is open from 10-5:30.*
*Tea is served from 11 to 4 and reservations are recommended, usually 1-2 days in advance. Groups are welcome.*

*Proprietor's*
*Autograph*_____*Date*_____

# Lady Di's British Store and Tea Room

*420 Second Street*
*Lake Oswego, Oregon 97034*
*503-635-7298 / 1-800-357-7839*
*www.britishfare.com*

*From I-5/217, take Kruse Way to Boones Ferry. Follow signs to downtown*
*Lake Oswego. From I-205, take Hwy 43 to West Linn then to Lake Oswego.*
*Left at A Ave. then right on 2nd.*

Lady Di, with it's convenient location, has been a mainstay in Lake Oswego for a number of years. The store shelves are stocked with an extensive selection of British groceries and teas and there are frozen and refrigerated items available for purchase.

Collectables, such as teapots, cards, miniatures, pictures and other English items are also there to tempt you.

Tucked away in a corner is the vine clad tea room, where one can enjoy a cup of tea and quiet conversation. Moya offers a varied menu from which one can select a tasty morsel to enjoy with the tea. You may choose a sandwich only with crisps and fruit for $4.75 or the Lady Di Tea which includes a tart, biscuits, shortbread, cake, fruit and a tea sandwich for $9.50. If you prefer a scone, there is a Devon Cream Tea for $9.95 which also includes fruit and tea sandwich. A holiday menu is offered between Thanksgiving and Christmas. Groups of 6 or more are charged a 20% gratuity.

MC/V                    Free Street Parking

*Store hours Mon.- Sat. 10-5. Teatime is from 11-4. There is seating for 12*
*people in the Garden area. A separate parlor seats 4-5. Reservations maybe*
*on Sat. and for groups of more than 6. Special TEAs for Mothers Day,*
*Valentine's Day, etc.*          *(see WEB page)*

*Proprietor's*
*Autograph*_____*Date*_____

# Lavender Tea House

## and Gift Shop

340 N.W. 1st Avenue
Sherwood, Oregon 97140
503-625-4479
LavenderTeaHouse@yahoo.com /
www.lavenderteahouse.com

*From I-5, take Tualatin/Sherwood Exit and go west on Tualatin Sherwood Road. Go left on Hwy 99, left at Sherwood Blvd and right on NW 1st Street. Located across from Veterans Park.*

The location of Lavender Tea House couldn't have been more suitably chosen...across from a park with a huge aging tree and at the end the street in a quaint neighborhood. As you drive up you feel as if you "have arrived" and this is going to be something special. The tea room is set up in a charming 1892 Queen Anne style Victorian Home and the theme is carried out in a "English cottage style" décor.

Two special teas are offered - the High Tea and Afternoon Tea. High Tea is an English style tea served in three courses. The first course is 6 tea sandwiches and soup followed by a scone with jam & clotted cream and fruit. The final course is dessert and this dessert is priced at $21.95. After-noon Tea is a refreshing afternoon's repast of 6 tea sandwiches, scone with jam & clotted cream, lemon curd, and dessert for $14.95. Tea and gratuity are    included in the above teas and prices are per person.

For the smaller appetite there are two other offerings on the Luncheon menu. Queen Mum has 4 tea sandwiches, scone with jam & clotted cream and afresh fruit for $7.75. The Garden has 4 tea sandwiches, fresh fruit and a truffle for $6.95. Tea is not included but is available at $2.00 for one and $3.00 for two. There is a children's tea for $5.75 as well as other lighter fare items. Outside catering us offered, too.

MC/V/Checks          Wheelchair Accessible          Free Street Parking

*Open Tuesday through Saturday 11-4. Tea time is 11-3:30.*
*Groups are welcome. The maximum is 30 people.*

*Proprietor's*
*Autograph*_____ *Date*_____

# Leach Botanical Garden

*6704 S.E. 122nd Avenue*
*Portland, OR. 97236*
*503-823-9503*
*pkdvanmeter@ci.portland.or.us*

*From I-5, take Foster Road exit East to 122nd Avenue. Turn rt. 1/4 mile to garden parking lot.*

Though teas are only offered twice a year, they are excellent and worth putting on your calendar now. On one weekend in March and one in July, Leach Garden offers a fundraising tea for $15.00 per person. Tea is served in three courses with a first course of scones with jam, Devonshire jam and butter patties. The second course might consist of such delectables as a fruit cup, asparagus rolls, dilly cucumber rounds, Persian chicken packets, and tomato with basil and mozzarella cheese. For a finale, perhaps you will be offered poppy seed cake, lemon curd tart, raspberry shortbread and chocolate truffle. What ever the menu, and it changes each time, you will be pleased with the taste and presentation. The dates for the 2004 teas are March 25 & 27 and July 14 & 15th and seatings are 12 and 2pm. The March tea will be served in the Manor House and the July tea in the Garden's East Terrace. Each table is uniquely decorated and the tea is graciously served by volunteers.

There is a gift shop so allow yourself a little extra time to look around after you have toured the gardens and enjoyed this wonderful tea.

MC/V/Checks          Wheelchair Accessible          Free Lot Parking

*The gardens are open 9-4 Tuesday through Saturday and 1-4 Sunday. Teas are offered twice a year, once in the spring and once in the summer, by reservation.*

*Proprietor's*
*Autograph_____Date_____*

# Mon Ami

490 Highway 101
Florence, Oregon 97439
541-997-9234
wobbe@presys.com

*From Hwy 126 E, turn left onto Hwy 101. They are located next to the Purple Pelican Antique Mall at the corner of Hwy 101 and Rhododendron.*

Mon Ami is among the many tea rooms making an appearance on the Oregon coast. A really adventurous soul could spend a couple of days just driving from one to the other while seeing the beautiful sights and listening to the wonderful sounds of the coast!

The tea room tables are located amid a wonderful collection of antiques and collectables, all of which will tempt you while waiting for tea to be served. Seems I never stay seated very long, as I find myself browsing between courses. Not to worry, Cindy never rushes you!

There are three tea sets from which to choose, starting with the cream tea of scones, shortbread, clotted cream and lemon curd for $3.95. The next offering is the Petite Luncheonette and it includes a delightful salad, two tea sandwiches (may include quiche if available), fresh scones and shortbread with lemon curd and clotted cream, and petite desserts. The High Tea, which is served in three courses and *requires reservations*, includes assorted tea sandwiches and canapés, their signature Waldorf salad, freshly baked scones with citrus curd, classic shortbreads, delicate desserts and a pot of tea for $12.95. Dietary needs may be accommodated with advance notice and they are "Adkins friendly"! The house tea is Taylors of Harrogate and they offer that, as well as other labels, for sale. Holiday teas are offered and they would be "happy to do special theme teas" for your special occasion.

This is a great area of town to do some browsing so allow yourself plenty of time to check out Mon Ami as well as the other stores around it.

MC/V/DIS/Checks                    Free Street and Lot Parking
Wheelchair accessible but please let them know you are coming.

*Open 9:30-5 Mon. through Fri. and 10-5 on Sat. Closed Sunday. Tea time is 1:30 - 4 or by appointment. Reservations are required 24 hours in advance for parties of 6 or less and 48 hours in advance for parties of 6 or more.*

Proprietor's
Autograph_____Date_____

# *Mrs. B's Special Teas*

*55 West Grant*
*Lebanon, Oregon 97355*
*541-259-5100*

*From I-5, go East on Hwy. 34 at Exit 238. Follow the highway into town. Go right when the road forks. Stay in the left hand lane then turn left at Grant Street and go about a block. You can't miss it!*

The lone Tudor style building on Grant Street beckons you to step inside and have a "cuppa". Barbara has dedicated the tea room to the memory of her very special mother, Gatha Viola, and her love of all things tea is evident in the food, ambiance and service.

Though delicious lunches and elegant weekend dinners are offered, tea time in the room in the corner, is her specialty. The color scheme changes monthly to suit that months holiday. Everything changes...table cloths, glassware, teapots, candles, dishes and even the many collectables which adorn the shelves above you that encircle the room.

The tiered servers, with the appropriate colored flowers, feature a special sandwich to match the theme! There are a number of tea offerings: the Royal Tea of scone and four desserts at $8.00, the Luncheon Tea with 2 tea sandwiches, scone and 4 desserts for $12.00, the four course Victorian Tea for $15.00 and the five course Queens tea at $18.00. The latter two feature five desserts! All include, Devon Cream, preserves and a pot of tea. Coffee is available.

I recommend that you plan to arrive early or stay late, because the gift area is very large and ever so interesting. You will find everything from cards, books and teapots to boas, hats and a "sea of red and purple". Take your time checking out because all the fun jewelry is near the cash register and you are bound to get distracted!

MC/V/Checks     Wheelchair Accessible     Street Parking and Lot

*The gift shop is open from 10-5:30 and lunch is served from 11-2. Reservations are **recommended** for the Luncheon tea but are **required** 48 hours ahead for the Queen and Victorian Teas, which must be pre-paid. Tea is offered on Wed-Fri. beginning at 1:30, and from 11-3 on Saturdays.*

*Proprietor's*
*Autograph*_____ *Date*_____

# Nauna's Tea Room
## at Mission Mill Museum

1313 Mill Street S.E.
Salem, Oregon 97301
503-370-8855 / fax 503-370-9844
www.millcreekstation.com

*Located at the Historic Mission Mill Museum*

Nauna's Tea Room is an annex of Mill Creek Station and Catering and is located within the Mission Mill Museum Complex. It is a separate glassed in room which sets you away from the hustle and bustle of the main dining area.

Mill Creek Station has a complete café menu with soup and sandwiches starting at $5.95. They offer scones and tea starting at $3.00 as well as other fresh made pastries and cookies. Tea is sold by the cup or by the pot at all times.

Special parties for 8 or more people may be arranged to celebrate a shower, birthday, retirement or any other special event. These may be luncheons or themed teas and they must be arranged in advance. Christmas Teas are sometimes offered, too.

There is a gift shop available for browsing.

MC/V/AE                Wheelchair Accessible                Parking Lot

*Monday to Friday 9-4 p.m.*
*Sunday 10-4 p.m.*
*Tea parities by appointment with an 8 person minimum*

*Proprietor's*
*Autograph*_____*Date*_____

# Newell House Museum

## at Champoeg State Park
St. Paul, Oregon 97137
503-678-5537
newellhsemuseum@aol.com

*From I-5 take exit toward Champoeg State Park. The house is on the left before you turn into the park main entrance.*

For those of us who like all things historical, the Robert Newell House is the perfect place to enjoy two important jewels of the past...traditional tea-time and an historic home. Owned by the Daughters of the Revolution, the home is a beautiful reminder of how things used to be, just as tea time is a reminder of what can be...a slower, gentler time. If you plan to visit the museum, invite a group of friends and enjoy an afternoon of tea and conversation in this wonderfully preserved 1850's farmhouse.

There are a number of different teas available ranging in price from the $12.00 Princess Tea consisting of tea, scones, and fruit to The Royal Tea which offers tea, 6 tea sandwiches, scone w/jam and clotted cream, fresh fruit and dessert for $21.00. The prices are for a minimum of 8 and include admission to tour the house. During the summer, teas may be held in the garden, on the tea porch or in the Great Room. During inclement weather teas are presented in the Great Room only. We had the pleasure of taking tea inside and it was such a perfect setting...seated at antique tables covered with vintage linens and wonderful old mis-matched china cups and saucers, surrounded by so many remnants of the past. Tea was served in courses and iced tea as well as hot tea was included.

During the course of the afternoon, our hostess Judy, gave detailed history of the house and it's relationship to the town of Champoeg. After a leisurely tea, we were able to ramble about the house taking in all the history it had to offer. How I loved the room full of inaugural dresses of former governors wives that dated back to the 1850's. To top off your visit, take a tour of the grounds and see the jail and school house that have been moved to the property.

Checks/Cash          Wheelchair Access only on the Porch          Lot Parking

*Tea is by appointment only. A two week deposit is required as is a 48 hour cancellation notice.*

*Proprietor's*
*Autograph*_____*Date*_____

# Once Upon a Time

*Central Point, Oregon 97502*
*541-665-2808*
*dressup@cdsnet.net*
*www.princessparty.com*

*Tea parties are presented at clients homes or other location.*

What better way to introduce little boys and girls to the fine art of taking tea than a personalized tea party? Teri does just that with her dreamy, dress-up tea parties for children which she calls "indulgent and elegant"!. She offers parties in your home, as well as for organizations at their location of choice. Children get to dress up in high quality costumes such as princesses (Royal Tea) or faux stoles and elegant vintage gowns, hats and jewelry (Sweet Tea). Teri also teaches etiquette classes with a tea party at the end of the session.

An example of a themed tea is A Royal Princess Dress-Me-Up Party, which offers costumes and accessories for children ages 4-7. The guest of honor is given royal attire and a throne, a crowning ceremony, a Princess parade, a royal ball, an official Princess certificate and a special gift. Guests will receive personalized invitations that are addressed and mailed for you. The following amenities will be provided; a bubble machine to greet the guests, an instant camera with photo frames, a royal table setting, a fabulous castle cake, ice cream, 7-up and party favors. You simply choose a date, supply the guest list and relax...the rest is done for you! There is a non-refundable deposit on all events and the cost of these all inclusive parties is based on the number of children.

Besides private parties, Once Upon a Time does the annual children's tea for the Voorhies Mansion and they are doing a Nutcracker Tea at the Craterian Theater for the Rogue Ballet in 2003.

MC/V/DIS/Checks       Special dietary needs can be accommodated.

*Most tea parties are held on Saturday and the most popular time is 1:00 p.m.*
*Two weeks advance reservation recommended.*

*Proprietor's*
*Autograph*_____*Date*_____

# The Oregon Tea Garden

*305 Oak Street*
*Silverton, Oregon 97381*
*503-873-1230 / fax 503-874-0906*
*oregonteagarden@aol.com*

*Follow signs to downtown Silverton. The tea room is located at 1ˢᵗ and Oak*
*Streets in the Silverton Realty Bldg. It is just ¾ mile from The Oregon*
*Gardens.*

This is one of those tea rooms that you just can't forget once you have
visited. From the outside, there are no clues to just how charming this little
oasis is. The bright yellow walls and upside down floral umbrellas, which
are hung from the ceiling, are off-set with beautiful white chair covers with
large lovely bows at the back. How can such a fun place be so elegant too?

Then...you select your tea offering and more surprises await you. Jennifer's generous use of fresh flowers and vegetable decors make the tea plates
works of art...almost too pretty to eat. But, do! Besides being attractive, the
food is delicious. High tea is a presentation of assorted tea sandwiches gar-
nished with fresh fruits, a medley of sweets (cake fit for a queen and the
worlds best bread pudding are among the selections), warm cream scones
and a pot of tea.

Besides High Tea, there is a selection of lunch entrees such as quiche,
salads, sandwiches, soup and of course, scones.

While dining, you will find yourself surrounded by an extensive gift shop. Stop to
check out the Spode China, gift baskets, tea
pots and handmade aprons and tea cozies as
well as assorted tea accoutrements.

MC/V/AE/DC/DIS          Wheelchair Access          Metered Parking

*Tuesday through Saturday 10-4. The tea room may be reserved on Sunday*
*or Monday for special occasions or private parties. They prefer reserva-*
*tions for groups of 5 or more.*

*Proprietor's*
*Autograph_____Date_____*

# The Primrose Tea Room

*334 Third Street*
*McMinnville, Oregon 97128*
*503-474-1559*

*99W to downtown McMinnville (Third Street). Turn east to the 300 block. The tea room is inside "The Book Shop". It is between Davis and Cowls Streets.*

What a surprise it was to find this tea room in the heart of downtown McMinnville! Though we had planned to take tea somewhere else, circumstances led us to this delightful spot and we were not disappointed. The British style tea room is situated in the back of a very large book store and it also shares space with The Red Berry, a small antiques business.

Though the tea area is small in size, the owner is big on hospitality. Our tea, which was PG Tipps Cut Black, came right away. As we enjoyed sipping it, we were able to chat with Richard as he prepared a very generous selection of sandwiches for us. They were served with coleslaw and fruit and were followed by a delicious scone and an assortment of desserts. The price range for teas is $3.45 for a cream tea to $10.95 for the full afternoon tea. The menu includes a few other luncheon items such as soup, house salad, chefs special and Shepherd's Pie. The soup is a wonderful specialty called Queen Victoria Soup and it is most unique and delicious. Do try it!

Special dietary needs accommodated with advance request.

Checks Accepted    2 hr. Metered Parking    Wheelchair Accessible

*Monday-Saturday 10-5. The kitchen closes at 4:30 p.m. Groups welcome with prior reservation.*

*Proprietor's*
*Autograph*_____*Date*_____

46

# Rose's Tea Room

*155 S.E. Vista Avenue*
*Gresham, Oregon 97080*
*503-665-7215*
*rosestroom@aol.com / www.rosesteroom.net*

*From I-84 East, take Exit 16. Turn right and go approximately 6 miles to*
*Powell Blvd. Turn right, then turn left immediately onto Vista Avenue. It is*
*near Sun Belt Rentals.*

Tucked away in a quaint neighborhood in Gresham sits this delightful
and charming tea house. Though it looks small from the outside, once you
are inside, you find that it grows with every step. We ventured all the way to
the back where we were seated at a table from which we could look out of
the windows and view the little flower garden outside. Cindy and Tonia say
that their tea room reflects "gracious living inspired by the 20's and 30's"
and that is reflected in the layered tablecloths, china cups and seasonal flowers that grace the tables, as well as the very friendly hospitality.

The menu choices are varied and there is something for everyone. Should
you be looking for something other than tea, you may choose the Ploughman's Plate, the Chicken Salad Luncheon, the Caribbean Chicken Salad or
the Earl Sandwich. The cost for any of those choices is $9.50 and it includes
fruit or a freshly made dessert, a scone and tea. As for tea sets, there are two
to choose from; the Tea Luncheon Plate, which offers a cranberry chicken
salad puff, assorted tea sandwiches, fresh fruit, dessert, a scone and tea for
$9.95 or the Royal High Tea, which is served in four course and consists of
soup and scones with jam and cream, assorted tea sandwiches and savories
with fresh fruit, dessert course and a chocolate course for $14.95. Of course,
this is the one we chose and it was delicious as well as attractively presented.
Soup can be added to any of the above for $1.00, there is a daily pasta
special and many of the items can be purchased separately. Also, low carb
options are available.

There is a small gift shop to tempt you while you wait to be seated or to
delay you on your way out! Take time to check it out!

MC/V/Checks          Wheelchair Accessible          Street and Lot Parking

*Hours are Tuesday through Saturday, 11-4. Reservations are not required*
*but are highly recommended on Saturdays.*

*Proprietor's*
*Autograph*_____*Date*_____

# Ruthie B's

*100 Main Street*
*Springfield, Oregon 97477*
*541-988-4791*

*From I-5, take exit 194A. Take the first Springfield exit-right on Pioneer*
*Parkway. Take another right on Main Street and continue to the tea room.*

This is so much more than a tea house! The owner, Ruth, describes it as "Fun with Tea and Art" but that barely begins to describe this amazing place. Just one word of warning, "allow yourself plenty of time when you stop here!".

Tables are placed among the antiques...here, there, and everywhere. It is such a friendly place, you never know who you will strike up a conversation with while enjoying your meal. Oh, and be sure to check out the "costume" area before settling in, as the perfect hat or outrageous boa may be calling you! Besides antiques of every kind, there are gift items scattered about the place, from candles and potpourri to Americana art and jewelry. As I said, "allow your self time to look".

Lunch fare such as sandwiches, soup, salads and Ruthie's own quiche are available. Meals change daily and most items are priced from $3.00 to $7.00.

The tea time offerings, which you can also enjoy in the most interesting garden, come in four sizes. The Tea with a Treat is offered with shortbread for $4.00, Tea with Cream comes with a scone with jam and imported Devon cream for $6.50 and the Garden Tea includes soup, tea sandwiches and a shortbread treat for $12.00. The very special High Tea offers tea sandwiches, soup, a savory, scone with jam and imported Devon cream, fruit compote and assorted tea desserts is $18.00 per person. Special teas are presented throughout the year including the Mad Hatters Tea and the 1930's Gurlfriend Tea Party featuring "Big Red" and the "Gurls". The latter is a clue to the tea rooms early residents! Remember...fun is the definitive word!

MC/V/AE/DC/DIS/MC/V/AE/DC/DIS/JCB
Garden is Wheelchair Accessible          Parking Lot

*Monday – Saturday 10-5:30 and Sunday 12-4*
*Tea is served all the hours they are open. Reservations are required on*
*Friday and Saturday and for parties of more than 6 people*

*Proprietor's*
*Autograph_____Date_____*

# *Savoure'*

*201 W. Broadway*
*Eugene, Oregon 97401*
*541-242-1010*
*cpotter@savouretea.com / www.savouretea.com*

*Savoure' is located at the corner of Charnelton and Broadway near the downtown district. Check the website for more information.*

If you have not visited a French tea room in the past, you will immediately sense the difference upon entering Savoure'. The rich red walls, floor to ceiling white drapery, huge picture windows, and many gold accents suggest that this tearoom visit is going to be different. Cindy has visited France many times and her attention to detail reflects those journeys. The beautiful samovar on the counter is the first thing to catch your eye. Then, as you wander around the corner, you see a wall that reaches to the ceiling with their signature tea selections from Mariage Freres, and a showroom that displays teapots, books, dishes and other necessities for the "tea lover".

Tea is served on small tables draped with crisp white linens. The beautifully upholstered chairs and couches are comfortable and inviting. Tables are set with white English china and the tea sets are presented on silver tiered plates with dainty silver servers.

The tea sets are numerous and include the Tart and Tea at $7.00, Proust's Tea, which consists of macaroons or 2 scones, for $5.50, Dessert tea for $8.75, Tea Savories $7.25, Very Nearly Tea for children at $7.00 and the Salon Tea for $15.00. A typical Salon tea would be bagelette with proscuitto and mozzarella, pastry puff with mushrooms and garlic, quiche with chives and cheddar, crostini with pesto, scones with clotted cream and jam, petit four, apple shortbread, chocolate macaroon and lemon and ginger teabread. The menu changes monthly and you can check their website each month to find out what that months offerings are going to be. One thing you can count on...it will be delicious and interesting!

MC/V/AE/DIS/MC/V/AE/DC/DIS/JCB
Wheelchair Accessible          Metered and Lot Parking

*Open Monday through Saturday 10-6 and Sunday 12-5. Tea is served until 1/2 hour before closing. They take reservations for parties of 7-10 people, Monday through Friday. Friday through Sunday is first come first served!*

*Proprietor's*
*Autograph*_____*Date*_____

# Shelton-McMurphey-Johnson House

*303 Willamette Street*
*Eugene, Oregon 97401*
*541-484-0808 / fax 541-984-1413*
*directon@smjhouse.org / www.smjhouse.org*

*From I-5 take Eugene/U of O exit - over the Ferry St.*
*Bridge. Go right on 3rd exit to Pearl Street. The house is*
*located off 3rd and Pearl.*

This is the perfect ambiance for afternoon tea...a stately Victorian mansion located in the heart of Eugene. The Shelton-McMurphey-Johnson house offers specialty teas in honor of Valentines Day, Mother's Day and Christmas. The traditional high tea menu may offer cucumber tea sandwiches, egg salad tea sandwiches, banana nut bread and cream cheese tea sandwiches, lemon tartlets, chocolate baby cakes, Madelines and mini scones with toppings. The tea offerings are catered in by some of the areas finest caterers and cost $15.00 per person. Since these teas are very popular, they fill up fast, so plan ahead and make reservations well in advance.

Private teas ranging from $5.00 to $15.00, depending on menu choices, are available with prior arrangements. You bring the group and they provide the ambiance and food! For those who prefer, coffee is available.

Dietary needs can be accommodated with prior arrangement.

Checks and Cash Only    Wheelchair Accessible    Parking Lot

*Holiday Tea's - February, May and December. Reservations required up to*
*1 month in advance. Cancellation policy. Private teas for groups of 5-30*
*people are also available.*

*Proprietor's*
*Autograph_____Date_____*

# *Sister Act Party Specialists*

## *Catering and Tea's*
*Corvallis, Oregon 97333*
*541-752-7624 / 541-757-6525*
*jacobt@onid.orst.edu / sisteractcatering@msn.com*

*Alicia and Deanna cater off site at your home or other location of your choice.*

As the name implies, Alicia and Deanna are sisters with a broad background in the catering business. They started at an early age helping their mother with her catering business then ventured out on their own when they became mothers themselves.

Though they do all types of catering, presenting tea's is their main focus. This duo has done a tea for as few as two people and as many as seventy-five. A typical afternoon tea includes sandwiches, savories, fruit, scones, assorted desserts and of course, tea. Other types of teas are available depending on your needs, and price is dependent on what type of tea you choose. The average range is $10.00 to $15.00. They also enjoy doing theme teas such as Mother's Day, Valentines Day, Christmas, Birthday Parties, Bridal and Baby Showers as well as your personal theme choice.

Additional items that they can provide for a minimal fee are linens, tableware, teapots and other tea accoutrements, dishes, and decorations.

Besides teas, Sister Act does catering for groups and individuals at the clients home or at another location. Call for prices and specific information.

*One weeks notice on teas is appreciated.*

*Proprietor's*
*Autograph*_____*Date*_____

# Tea and Tomes, Ltd.

*716 N.W. Beach Drive*
*Newport, Oregon 97365*
*541-265-2867 / 888-T-N-TOMES*
*mail@virtualtea.com / www.virtualtea.com*

*At the Hwy. 20/101 intersection, go west to Coast Street. Turn right on Coast then left on Beach Drive. The tall Tudor style building on the right is your destination.*

What a surprise we encountered as we first stepped inside this charming English style tea room. There was an immediate sense that this was going to be a special afternoon, as we noticed the servers in their long black skirts, crisp white blouses and period style white aprons The room was dressed in linen clad tables, lace touches, pre-set cups and saucers and an eclectic collection of tables and chairs. Tea themed pictures, little shelves with books and other small items adorned the walls. Dawn always has a charming centerpiece on each table that makes you wish you were a little more talented or creative!

The house tea is Tuppence Tea, their own line, and the selection is extensive. Once seated, your order is taken and tea is served in a timely manner. We always choose the Classic Tea which consists of sorbet, 4 tea sandwiches, savories, scones, fresh fruit and 3 desserts, including the signature 'teapot cake', for $11.95. Other selections are available and the prices are $6.50 and $6.95. The Fairy Tale Tea for children is $6.95.

You won't want to leave and luckily the extensive gift shop will help to delay your departure. Take your time...there is so much to see!

MC/V/DIS/Checks     Street & Lot Parking
Wheelchair Access

*Hours of operation are Tuesday through Saturday from 11 to 5 p.m. No teas are served after 4:30 p.m.* **The tearoom is closed the entire month of January.** *Reservations needed for 6 or more.*

*Proprietor's*
*Autograph*_____ *Date*_____

# The Tea Cosy

*95 W. 11th Avenue*
*Bandon, Oregon 97411*
*541-347-4171*
*jane@theteacosy.com*

Come for tea & stay awhile!

*From Hwy. 101, in Uptown Bandon, turn west at the light by Bank of America. The tea room is right behind the bank.*

Jane had a dream and she turned it into a reality with the opening of her proper British tea room. As her brochure states, "In the British Isles, tea can be a beverage, a snack or a meal-it is always a relaxing break in the day, especially when shared with friends".

When you relax at The Tea Cosy, you have the opportunity to partake of one of the many tea offerings, from a Cream Tea at $5.75 to a full High Tea at $18.75. The High Tea offers cottage garden salad, hearty soup, quiche or frittata, finger sandwiches, tea breads and sweets, scones and fresh fruit. The Cambric tea for children is $4.75 for one or $7.75 for two. Some dietary needs can be accommodated with advance notice. All teas include a pot of tea made from the extensive selection of loose-leaf teas.

There is a full lunch menu, however coffee is not offered. Special Sunday brunches and Tea Parties are available as well. Call for specifics. There is a gift shop on the premises.

MC/V/AE/DIS/Checks     Wheelchair Accessible     Free Parking

*Summer hours (effective Memorial Day) open daily 10-5*
*Winter hours (effective Labor Day) Wednesday through Saturday 10-5 and Sundays noon to 5. Reservations are required for groups of 5 or more.*

*Proprietor's*
*Autograph_____Date_____*

# Tea Events

*702 N.E. Norton*
*Bend, Oregon 97701*
*541-382-5515*
*tea@teaevents.com / www.teaevents.com*

*Directions will be made available when reservations are confirmed.*

This is a special tea offering, which we first found on the inter-net. The home page was so interesting that we just had to know more about Tea Events. We contacted the owner, Dawnya Sasse, and started an online correspondence feeling like we had found a new "tea" friend!

Tea Events is a specialized business which offers tea to private parties of 5 or more by appointment, as well as themed teas which are open to the public by reservation. Every tea is unique and is custom made for the occasion. Groups may reserve the entire tea house, with its Victorian atmosphere and beautiful amenities, for their private party. The cost is $12.00 to $20.00 per person, depending on the tea menu. The events, which are open to the public, always have a theme, which is carried out right down to the minutest detail. Contact Dawnya for more information or check her website for updates.

Children's events are available, along with class on manners and etiquette. Full dress-up teas are especially popular with young girls and their mothers. There is definitely something for everyone in this unique setting.

MC/V/DIS/Checks     Free Parking
Wheelchair Accessible

*Tea is by reservation only with a 48 hour advance notice and times vary by event. Cancellation is also within 48 hours or non-refundable deposit is forfeited.*

*Proprietor's*
*Autograph_____Date_____*

# The Tea Zone

*51 N.W. 11ᵗʰ Avenue*
*Portland, Oregon 97209*
*jasmine@teazone.com / www.teazone.com*

*1-5 to 405 N(299B)  Take exit 2B to Everett St. The exit will merge onto 14ᵗʰ Ave. Follow 14ᵗʰ about 4 blks to Hoyt St and turn Rt. Go to 11ᵗʰ St. and turn left. The shop is on the left side.*

Located in the Historic Pearl District, The Tea Zone offers over 65 loose leaf teas, bearing their own label, and ranging in price from $2.00 to $7.00 per ounce. If you are looking for prepared tea, it can be purchased at $2.65 - $3.70 for a one person pot and $4.30 to $6.40 for a two person pot. To accompany your beverage, you can purchase scones (they say the best in town!), breads, muffins, cookies, desserts and other treats.

This European style establishment also offers hardier fare, and the choices are numerous. They include empanadas, galettes, pasties, quiche, grilled panini sandwiches and a Southwest tuna sandwich. These entrees range in price from $2.25 to $5.95 and a mixed greens side salad may be added for $1.75. Daily specials are also available. When possible, dietary needs can be accommodated.

For those of us who enjoy the event called "Tea Time", monthly High Teas and Holiday High Teas are offered.

MC/V/AE/DIS/Checks       Gift Shop       Wheelchair Accessible
Metered street parking and a self-serve pay lot are available.

*Weekdays open at 8:00 a.m.. / Weekends open at 10:00 a.m.*
*Sun-Wed - close at 6:00 p.m. / Thurs-Sat-close at 8:00 p.m.*
*Call for dates and times of High Tea events.*

*Proprietor's*
*Autograph_____Date_____*

# Tracy Hill Home & Garden

*223 S.E. Davis Avenue*
*Bend, Oregon 97701*
*541-319-9245*
*atracydesign@aol.com*

*From Hwy 97, turn onto Davis Avenue. It's the very first street south of the*
*railroad underpass. Coins and Collectables Shop is around the corner.*

Tracy Hill has the most interesting atmosphere for an afternoon tea...you can shop while you sip! Tea is served on mismatched vintage dishes with old linens, and odd silverware. The tables are located in several rooms, laden with retail merchandise, in an old bungalow style house. Everything is for sale, even the chair you are sitting upon! What a concept, shop without having to leave the table.

The tea set is catered by "Tea Events of Bend". Fall teas are preceded by a free "tea talk" at 11:30 titled, Planning a Holiday Tea, by Lady Dawnya Sasse. Groups are welcome with a minimum of 12 and a maximum of 24.

The menu varies but always includes a scone, soup, savories, "fussy little sandwiches" and sweets, presented on tiered servers, for $12.50. The sandwiches are too pretty to eat...but please do! The theme and decorations for the tea are appropriate to the month. The house tea is "Lavender Lane". It is blended especially for Tracy Hill, and is available for purchase.

Tracy Hill is home base for Bend's "Women With Hattitude" chapter of the RHS and owner, Tracy, will arrange special tea times for Red Hatters.

Visitors are always greeted with a steaming cup of tea on Tuesdays and Wednesdays. What a pleasant way to browse, especially on those chilly winter days.

MC/V/Checks     Not Wheelchair Accessible
Free Street Parking

*Open Tuesday through Saturday 10-6. Teatime is the second Tuesday of*
*each month at 1:00 p.m. Reservations are required one week ahead and the*
*cancellation policy is 24 hours.*

*Proprietor's*
*Autograph_____Date_____*

# Tudor Rose Tea Room

*480 Liberty Street S.E.*
*Salem, Oregon 97301*
*503-588-2345*

*From I-5, take the Mission St. (Hwy 22) exit and go to Liberty St. Turn right, go a few blocks, and watch for the tea room on the right. From Hwy 99, go across the bridge and turn right on High St. Go past the hospital and take the next right. Proceed to Liberty and take another right. The tea room is just down the street on the right hand side of the street.,*

Located in the back of an attractive English Tudor Style building, Tudor Rose Tea Room is a charming and comfortable place to take tea or any of the other afternoon lunch items that are offered. The real challenge is getting to the back! You must first pass through one of the most tempting gift shops in the area. There are so many tea-related items that it is difficult to choose just which ones you "can't live without". There are many other "necessities" to numerable to describe, as well. For those who like a bit of England, Bob carries a large selection of British foods to tempt the palate. Of course, those are to take home, because, after you have enjoyed the generous tea, you won't be able to taste another morsel.

The full afternoon tea consists of a first course salad or savory served with traditional English sandwiches. This is followed by a generous scone, then trifle or other special pudding. To end the meal, a tiered server brings a sampling of delicious desserts and a chocolate dipped strawberry. The price of the full tea is $11.95. There is also a smaller luncheon tea for $7.25.

V/MC/Dis/Checks          Wheelchair Accessible          Lot Parking

*The shop is open 11-5:30 Mon. through Fri., 11-5 on Sat. and 12-4 on Sun. Afternoon Tea is by reservation. Days vary so call for specifics. The luncheon tea is always available. Groups are welcome by advance reservation.*

*Proprietor's*
*Autograph*_____*Date*_____

# Wakai Tea Room

1633 S.W. Skyline Boulevard
Portland, Oregon 97221
503-242-1557

*Located in the Sylvan Area in SW Portland - call for directions*

Tea and Inspiration is offered once a month, usually on a Sunday, in this 8 mat Japanese Tea Room, located in a private home. The suggested donation is $15.00 and reservations are required one week in advance.

June serves a Japanese sweet and a bowl of Matcha, which is a high quality powdered green tea, and the experience is reflective of the season. In the quiet setting of a garden and teahouse, guests contemplate words on a scroll, view the flowers in the alcove and enjoy a bowl of tea

Chado, the way of tea, is the practice of preparing, serving and drinking tea. This elegant yet simple practice reflects the philosophy of the four principles of tea: Harmony (Wa), Respect (Kei), Purity (Sei) and Tranquility (Jaku).

Also, the teachers of the Wakai Tea Assn. host a Guest Evening on the last Tuesday of each month at the Wakai Tea Room. Donation is $10.00 per person. Private group experiences and lessons are available through the Urasenke Certified Teachers of Wakai.

Checks Accepted                    Off Street Parking

*All teas by reservation only*

*Proprietor's*
*Autograph*_____*Date*_____

# The Wild Rose Tea Room

*422 S.W. 6th Street*
*Redmond, Oregon 97756*
*541-923-3385*

*They are located on the "downtown" portion of SW 6th Street, between SW Deschutes Avenue and SW Evergreen Street. 6th Street is a one way going South.*

Miss Bessie, the owner, invites you to "slip off the rush of your day and have a properly brewed pot of tea". That is exactly what we are all looking for in our pursuit of tea rooms!

The ambiance is American-English-Victorian and there are numerous menu choices to please those looking for a break, lunch or afternoon tea. If you are not in a hurry, there is also a gift and antique area for your shopping pleasure.

The lunch choices include soups, salads and beef pasties priced from $2.75 to $10.50. Ala carte scones may be ordered with any of the above or you may choose to try the Daily Dessert for $1.00 to $3.50.

Tea offerings include the Cream Tea for $8.50, the Sweet Tea for $11.95 and the Tea Luncheon, which consists of a warm scone with butter and strawberry jam, assorted tea sandwiches and fruit for $10.50. All include a pot of tea. The High Tea, which requires reservations, includes a scone with all the trimmings, a plate of assorted tea sandwiches, an assortment of savories, fruit "to clear the palate" and the grand finale of miniature desserts for $21.95.

Private parties of 20-40 people are welcome.

MC/V/DC/DIS/JCB/Checks    Wheelchair Access    Free Street Parking

*Days of operation are Tuesday through Saturday. The shop is open from 10-5 and food service is available from 11-4. High Tea, which is served Wed-Sat., requires a 24hr. advance reservation, and there is a minimum number.*

*Proprietor's*
*Autograph_____Date_____*

# Welcome
# to
# Washington

# A Touch of Elegance

*508 W. Bell Lane*
*St. John, Washington 99171*
*509-648-3466 / fax 509-648-3726*
*jfk@StJohncable.com.*

*St. John is south of Spokane - 14 miles off highway 195 and three miles from the Iris Test Gardens.*

Soft pink floral tablecloths, lace accessories and servers in white starched aprons greet you as you enter this charming Victorian style tea room. These are some of the special touches that Barb offers to those looking for gracious hospitality for their special event. Not just a tea room, but also a place to have a memorable luncheon, your friends and family will be treated to something special, from the ambiance to the food.

A catered lunch consisting of two menu items of your choice: soup, salad or dessert for $20.00 per person including tax and gratuity. If you choose to have soup, salad and dessert, the cost is $25.00. Sorbet and bread are included in meals. With so many soup and salad choices, choosing will be a challenge! Everything, including the breads, is made from scratch.

Tea time offers a wonderful Victorian Tea which includes scones, heart-shaped sandwiches, quiche, heart-shaped cheeses, sorbet, truffle, carrot cake, pecan tart, fancy sugar cookies and seasonal tarts. Assorted jams and jellies, spun honey butter and Devon cream are also served with the scones. All this for $25.00 including tax and gratuity.  Special themed teas are offered for holidays and birthdays and special dietary needs can be accommodated upon advance notice. Coffee is available.

After dining, guests are invited to browse through the Creative Workshop Boutique which features gifts and fine furnishings.

Checks/Cash          Not Wheelchair Accessible          Parking Lot

*Hours are 11-4 Mon. through Sat. Reservations are required with a minimum of 6 and maximum of 18.* **For the months of May and June, reservations need to be made 2 months in advance.** *Large groups require a one week cancellation. All groups are responsible for the number reserved unless cancellation is made 48 hours in advance.*

*Proprietor's*
*Autograph_____ Date_____*

# *Abby Garden Tea Room*

*1308A-11ᵗʰ Street*
*Bellingham, Washington 98225*
*360-752-1752*

*I-5 North - take the Fairhaven Exit and turn L. Turn R at 2ⁿᵈ light (12ᵗʰ St).*
*Go 2 blks. to light (Ham's St). Turn L, go 1 blk. then turn L onto 11ᵗʰ St. You*
*will be in the Fairhaven Historic District.*

We were determined to take tea at Abby Gardens and it was well worth
the adventure trying to find the Fairhaven Historic District where it is located. We didn't have directions!

This tea room is situated upstairs, almost in a loft like setting, over a
'paint your own' ceramic studio. Once seated, though, you enter the world of
a friendly neighborhood tea room. Scones are plated and are served with
your tea. The sandwiches and fruit are presented on tiered servers and desserts are served last. The tea selections are numerous and Anne offers over
50 types of tea, many of which are available for purchase. The tea time
selections range from $6.95 to $14.95.

Coffee and lunch items such as soup, sandwiches, salads, savories,
quiche and desserts are also on the menu. A gift shop shares the downstairs
space.

MC/V/Local Checks Only
Wheelchair accessible
Free street parking
Free municipal parking lot

*Tea is served Tues to Sunday 11 – 6. The last seating is at 4:30 p.m. Closed*
*Monday and holidays. Reservations are accepted for parties of 5 or more*
*and a party room will open in Fall '03.*

*Proprietor's*
*Autograph*_____*Date*_____

# All About Tea

*Cyrilla Gleason*
*360-690-1811*
*cyrilla4tea@yahoo.com*

*The location for the etiquette class will be determined at the time of booking.*

Cyrilla Gleason is a trained and certified Tea Etiquette Consultant and is the founder and director of *All About Tea*, a company specializing in tea education and etiquette. Classes, tea tutorials, and programs for groups are customized to the needs of the client. Mrs. Gleason has a BA in Education and is a certified teacher. She is a member of the Colonial Williamsburg Foundation and is a graduate of the Protocol School of Washington in McLean, Virginia, the leader in etiquette and protocol services.

*All About Tea* classes provide an entertaining opportunity for men, women and young people to learn proper etiquette for taking tea in business and social situations. As Mrs. Gleason states, "taking tea provides a special opportunity to spend quality time with friends, family, and associates".

Programs include the history of tea, the proper preparation of tea, and the etiquette used while taking tea. Antique tea items and new tea accessories are demonstrated in their use of preparing tea. You will learn how to make a perfect cup of Green, Oolong, and Black Tea and why incorrectly prepared tea is bitter. Programs and classes may be held in teashops, churches, businesses, clubs or homes.

Samples of programs are Afternoon Tea, High Tea, Friendship Tea and Etiquette, Traveling Tea Basket, Victorian or Colonial Days, Young Men's Manners, and Teddy Bear Tea and Etiquette. There is also a program for Church and Civic Organizations which is perfect for Brunch, lunch, tea or dinner meetings and can be given with or without a devotional.

For more information or to arrange a program, call or email Cyrilla.

*Classes are pre-arranged by reservation.*

*Proprietor's*
*Autograph*_____*Date*_____

# Althea's Tea Lounge

614 S. 1st. Street
Mount Vernon, Washington 98273
360-336-0602
jghlaw@yahoo.com / www.altheas.com

*Take I-5 to Exit 226 (Kincaid Street) and go west to S. First Street. Take a right and Althea's is on the right, halfway down the block. The tea room is just past Historic Pine Square.*

When I saw the sign, "any time is tea time", I knew that this would be my kind of place because...that is just how I think! This is also a place where relaxation seems to be the theme, with it's casual and welcoming atmosphere. The room is informal, with overstuffed chairs and couches as well as glass topped tables. A converted bar serves as their "tea bar".

Jennifer serves a tea plate that consists of tea sandwiches, scones, and shortbread cookies as well as lunch fare. The lunch menu includes sandwiches, wraps, soup, Gardenburgers and assorted salads for $3.95-$6.95. Special dietary needs can be accommodated upon request.

To accompany your meal, beverage choices abound. Specialty drinks are: real fruit and tea smoothies, ice cream shakes, fruit tea shakes and chai shakes. The house teas are Harney & Sons and Golden Moon but there are a number of other labels to choose from. They sell their teas in bulk and if they don't have your favorite, they will special order it for you.

Before leaving, be sure to stop at the gift shop for a little browsing. There you will find bath and tea items to purchase for yourself or as a gift for someone special. If you have the time, tanning beds and a massage therapist are at your disposal. Just be sure to call ahead for an appointment!

I have heard on good authority, the Mayor, that this is a great place to get away from it all so, when in the neighborhood, take time to take tea.

MC/V/Checks          Wheelchair Accessible          On Street Parking

*Open Mon-Fri 8-6:30 and Saturdays 9-5. Anytime is tea time! A seven day advance notice is required for Theme Teas or groups of 6 or more.*

Proprietor's
Autograph_____Date_____

# Anna's Tea Room

*606 N. Main Street*
PO Box 621
Coupeville, Washington 98239
360-678-5797

*From Route 20, turn onto North Main Street. They are*
*on North Main between 6th and 7th on the left side as*
*you drive toward the water. They are next to the*
*United Methodist Church on 7th and Main.*

How appropriate to find a tea room which honors the 7th Duchess of
Bedford who started it all for us! This charming 1903 Victorian home, with
it's shuttered windows, expansive front porch and white picket fence does
just that. Great detail was given to decorating the house by the owners, Lu
Anne and Kristin, and they chose shades of ivory, green and white to set off
the many antiques that fill their home. Anna's, which opened in the spring of
2002, is the perfect setting for tea

Customers first select their tea cup from a glass case filled with both antique and modern pieces. They are then seated at a table, or if they prefer, a
lush settee or an elegant Victorian chair, in the bright and cheery parlour.
The tea sets, which are served on antique china, range in price from the
Light Tea of scone with cream & jam and a slice of tea bread with lemon
curd for $5.75 to Anna's Royal Tea, which includes six tea sandwiches,
scone with cream and jam, slice of tea bread with lemon curd and choice of
sweet for $14.95. For an additional dollar, Anna's Luncheon Tea includes a
teacup of soup or choice of salad. If you prefer just sandwiches, The Earl for
$7.95 is perfect or if you are taking children to tea, Auntie Anna's School-
room Tea is available for $4.95. Special theme teas are presented throughout
the year and guests are given quizzes, which relate to the theme of the tea,
after picking out their tea cup. This is just for fun and is optional, but it does
make for some fun conversation and prizes are awarded to the winners!

If a tea set is not what you are looking for, soups, salads, lunch plate du
jour and sandwich du Jour are available. The tea items may be purchased a
la carte. Catering is available, including picnics with advance notice.

MC/V/Checks       Not Wheelchair Accessible       Free Street Parking

*Open Mon and Wed through Sat. 11-5 and Sun. 12-5. Closed Tuesdays. Any*
*time is tea time! Reservations are not required, however, they are happy to*
*take them and they are recommended for parties of 6 or more.*

*Proprietor's*
*Autograph*_____*Date*_____

# *Attic Secrets Tea Room & Gifts*

*4229 76ᵗʰ Street N.E.*
*Marysville, Washington 98270*
*360-659-7305*

*I-5 to exit 200. From north turn rt., go to*
*State Ave., turn rt., go to 76ᵗʰ(light). Turn*
*left, it's ½ block on left side next to Van Dam*
*Floors. From south, same except turn left off*
*exit, go accross overpass.*

This is one of Snohomish Counties oldest tea rooms and it has been selected one of the "top 10 places to dine" out of 200 restaurants. Owners
Happi and Rick's charming tea room, which they purchased in 1998, is a
decorators dream. They refer to it as "Hollywood Romantic". The rooms
carry out a different theme, and we really couldn't pick a favorite, since each
has something different to offer. One has Waverly Print table cloths, fresh
flowers, tulle wrapped chairs, white china and flowing floral draperies while
another takes you outdoors with it's "shuttered inside windows", brick wall
and wonderful murals. They do look a bit like something you would see on
the silver screen...perfect rooms with all the finishing touches!

Not to be outdone by the ambiance, the tea choices are something special, too. Happi offers everything from the Buttercup Tea with soup and
scone for $5.95 to the Grand Lady Tea which consists of scone, four tea
sandwiches and a specialty dessert for $13.95. Afternoon tea consists of a
scone, sweets and fruit for $6.95 and Primrose tea includes a scone, two tea
sandwiches fruit and sweets for $9.95. There
are more tea choices including the 'Little Dar-
ling' for children priced at $5.95, and chil-
dren's birthday parties are welcome. Tea is
included in all the menu choices and there are
35 different teas to choose from. Dietary needs
can be accommodated with advance notice.

There is a large gift shop for your browsing
pleasure.

A lunch menu is also available as are fresh  baked scones made to order.

Wheelchair Accessible                                  Lot and street parking.

*The shop is open Monday-Friday 10:30-5:00 and Saturday 10:30-4:00.*
*Reservations are recommended. Walk-in's are welcome, thought there may*
*be a little wait.*

*Proprietor's*
*Autograph_____Date_____*

# The Brambleberry Cottage
## and Tea Shoppe
*122 N. Argonne Road*
*Spokane, Washington 99212*
*509-455-8337*

*From the freeway, take the Argonne exit. Head So. and go through 2 lights (Mission then Broadway). From the left lane, turn into the parking lot at the bottom of the hill, just past Main.*

Melanie and Dawn have combined their experiences to offer those of us who think tea time is a "necessity", just what we are looking for. The Victorian Cottage décor welcomes you while flowers, greenery and the eclectic décor make you feel right at home. They offer tea as it is intended to be- a step back from your busy life to a time when things were simpler and people enjoyed afternoon indulgences.

The list of teas offerings is extensive, from the Cream Tea to the High Tea and includes a special one for children. All offer a choice of tea, and range in price from $5.00 to $18.50. Traditional cucumber as well as chicken almond, artichoke bruchetta, and ham and Swiss are among the sandwich choices. Desserts vary as well.

The ladies traditionally have a theme tea once a month that consists of an entirely different menu to fit the theme of the tea. Their house tea is Cottage Blend but they offer other teas. Coffee and special dietary needs may be requested in advance.

While there, take time to check out the gift and antique area and ask about the classes that are offered.

MC/V/Checks        Wheelchair Accessible        Street and Lot Parking

*Shop hours are Monday to Friday 10-6 and Saturday 10-5. Afternoon tea is served by appointment only, Tuesday through Saturday from 12-4.*

*Proprietor's*
*Autograph*_____*Date*_____

# The Brits

*1427 Commerce Avenue*
*Longview, Washington 98632*
*360-575-8090*

*From I-5 take exit 432 and proceed into town. Take a right at 15th then a right on Maple. Go one block and turn right on Commerce. From the Oregon side, cross the bridge and stay on Oregon Way. Turn Right on Hudson and left on Commerce.*

We were traveling north on one of our tea tours when we stopped in Longview to try this tea room. We were so glad we did! The room, with its distinctive British feel, was warm and inviting. Eclectic tables and chairs, crisp linens, an elevated fireside area and hats galore add to its charm. Joy, who has owned the tea room for six years, was very friendly and the service was efficient and timely.

The High Tea tables were covered with linens and fine china and the tea set was presented on tiered servers. The tea menu included sandwiches, scones, pastries, fruit and desserts for $12.95 plus gratuity. The scones were delicious, and were accompanied by double Devon cream and very tasty jam. Delicious Maids of Honor and Almond Oysters rounded out the selection of desserts. Tea time was leisurely and memorable!

Special theme teas and holiday teas, such as Christmas, Valentines and Mothers Day, are offered by reservation. Call for more information. A nice assortment of lunch entrees are also offered and those we saw looked wonderful!

After tea, take time to do a little shopping in the gift area. On one wall is a nice array of British foods and a selection of English teas. Beautiful tea pots as well as cup and saucer sets are available for purchase along with other tea accoutrements.

For a photo op, be sure to check out the red phone booth in the front of the store!

MC/V/Local Checks     Wheelchair Accessible     Street and Lot Parking

*The shop is open 11-4 Monday through Friday. High tea is offered by reservation in the late afternoon. Groups are welcome but please, not between the hours of 1 and 2.*

*Proprietor's*
*Autograph*_____*Date*_____

# *Carnelian Rose Tea Co.*

*1803 Main Street*
*Vancouver, Washington 98660*
*360-573-0917*
*tea@carnelianrosetea.com*
*www.carnelianrosetea.com*

*Directions - Take I-5 to Vancouver City Center and go west. At Main St., go right to 1803 Main. It is near the Clark County Historical Museum.*

Supplying wholesale signature tea blends to tea rooms, the Carnelian rose Tea Co. has a tea, antique and gift store which is now located in Uptown Village. A recent move gives the owner, Jennifer, 5500 square feet of well used space where the West Coasts premier Tea Business School is conducted. She is planning a second location in 2005. Tea samples are always available and tea luncheons are by reservation. Keeping with the theme of Uptown Village, the tea shop also houses a horseless carriage that is perfect for photo ops! Jennifer says, "my shop is a non-gender specific place where fancy laces and down home denims are both welcome".

Summertime seating is on the front porch amongst the botanicals while winter weather asks you to step inside the cheery interior of the tea shop. Only the finest grades of specialty teas are served, and teacups and teapots are an eclectic assortment which may be purchased to take home.

For a truly special treat, a full afternoon tea is available by reservation. Having experienced it, I can only say, "Get together a group of friends". The cost is from $9.95 to $18.95 and everything is made just for your event. A catering service is also available. Call for details.

Tea wares, antiques, fine art, hats and jewelry fill the gift shop area. Featured artists are Kenneth Ray Wilson and Aquila Art Glass.

MC/V/AE/DC/DIS/Checks          Wheelchair Access          Free Parking

*Open Monday through Saturday 10 to 4. Tuesday and Friday open until 6.*
*<u>48 hour advance reservations</u> required for afternoon tea. Groups are welcome.*

*Proprietor's*
*Autograph_____Date_____*

# The Cheshire Cat Tea Cottage

*2801 Fort Vancouver Way*
*Vancouver, Washington 98661*
*360-735-1141*

*From I-5 either direction, take the Fourth Plain Bl. exit*
*and head east. Turn left on Ft. Vancouver Way and pro-*
*ceed to red stop sign. The shoppe will be immediately*
*on the right corner.*

This is a charming British style tea room with royal family memorabilia adorning the walls, floral toppers on pastel tablecloths, and long lace window coverings crowned with silk greenery. The owner, Janet, calls herself a 'real British girl" and the tea room reflects her heritage. She offers tea to young and old alike and walk-in's are welcome except for High Tea.

Tea offerings are numerous, from tea and scones for $4.50 to the Lady Avril Tea which includes tea, an assortment of tea sandwiches, savory, fresh fruit, scone with jam & cream and dessert for $11.95. Nice to see the former owner, Avril, remembered with her own tea, however, reservations are required for that one. The house tea is Yorkshire Red but there are other label choices.

Light lunches are also offered such as Scotch meat pie, Ploughman's lunch and Cornish pastry with baked beans. There are also a few dessert items to tempt you. Carry out is available.

Gift items, most of which are imported, abound in the tea room so be sure to allow yourself time to look around.

MC/V/Local Checks     Wheelchair Access     Free  Parking Lot

*Shoppe is open Tues. through Sat. 11:00 to 5:00. Tea time is 11 to 4. Reser-*
*vations are required 48 hours in advance for **high tea**, prepaid only. After*
*4:00, tea and scones only.*

*Proprietor's*
*Autograph*_____*Date*_____

# Christine's Tea Cottage

*735 Burlington Blvd.*
*Burlington, Washington 98233*
*360-757-4889*
*chris@christinesteacottage.com*

*From I-5, take exit 230 and go east to Burlington Blvd. The tea room is on the right a few blocks down.*

Not far from the freeway, situated on the main street of town, sits this warm and welcoming cottage tea room. Christine, who opened the establishment in 2002, calls it a "magical and relaxing atmosphere", and we have to concur. The three rooms offer a different feel, from the more formal front room to the fun and colorful party room. Everywhere you look there is beautiful stenciling...over the doors, up the walls and around the room! Each room is brightened by windows dressed in lace and different hued tablecloths with lace toppers. Even the lovely ribbon bedecked menu's, which hold a wealth of information about tea, tea time and tea classes, show the attention to detail.

There are five tea sets available starting with the cream tea, which includes a scone and soup or a garden salad, for $7.95. The next three teas, named for Christine's daughters are: Stephanie's Little Friends Tea which consists of a scone with an assortment of two tea sandwiches, sweets and fruit for $7.95, Madison's Sweets and Tea for $9.95 and Alexandra's Best Friends Tea which offers a scone, assortment of four tea sandwiches, sweets and fruit for $12.95. The final tea is the Victorian Delight which includes choice of soup or garden salad, scone, assortment of four tea sandwiches,

sweets and fruit. All the tea include Devon Cream, lemon curd, jam and a pot of tea. The presentation was very pretty and the scones, large and delicious! Fresh made soups as well as sandwiches and a large selection of teas are available all day.

Christine also offers etiquette classes, readings and seminars.

MC/V/Checks          Wheelchair Accessible          Parking Lot

*Open Tuesday through Saturday 11-4 and tea is served all day. Reservations are recommended for groups of 4 or more. Theme teas that are offered are Ann of Green Gables, Fairy Tea, American Girl and Tea with Mrs. Claus.*

*Proprietor's*
*Autograph_____Date_____*

# Country Cottage Tea Parties

*12645 N.E .68th Place*
*Kirkland, Washington 98033*
*425-827-3366*

*From 405 take exit 17. Head E. on 70th to 128th and turn right. Go 1 block to NE 68th Pl. and turn right. It's the first house on the left. Bridle Trails Shopping Center is 2 blocks east.*

There is nothing like a tea party to make a person feel really special. I don't know if it's the idea of it or actually the event itself, but no matter...I love a tea party!

Pam offers many choices for her special tea parties, which she serves in the Victorian atmosphere of her own home. Inside seating offers a cozy setting, while an outside tea is presented in a gazebo with a waterfall and children's play house nearby.

Tea time offers an Adult Tea for $14.50 and it includes tea sandwiches, scones, fancy cookies, pastries, fruit and tea. Soup may be added for $2.00. The Child's Tea Party Package is $18.95 and it consists of a variety of tea sandwiches, scones, fruit, individual cakes and tea or lemonade. Dress up clothes, games, May-pole and croquet are offered as is the enchanting playhouse with heat and lights. Party favors for each child include a child's ceramic tea cup, sugar cubes and a silver spoon done up in tulle netting. The individual child's tea, which is $10.95, includes a variety of tea sandwiches, scones, fruit, individual cakes and tea or lemonade. Pam's special themed tea, the American Girl "Samantha" Tea is offered at $13.95 and has a variety of tea sandwiches, scones, fruit, individual cakes and tea or lemonade as well as American Girl pins and balloons. American Girl doll clothes, accessories and books are available for purchase.

Crafts are available for adults and children's teas at an additional charge. Other items for sale are a child's size tea cup and saucer for $5.00, a silver spoon for $3.50 and sugar cubes for $1.00.

Checks Accepted        Not Wheelchair Accessible        Street Parking

*Open Monday through Saturday by appointment only. Tea is usually served at 11:30 but that can be negotiated. Reservations are required at least one week in advance and there is a 4 day cancellation policy.*

*Proprietor's*
*Autograph*_____*Date*_____

# Elizabeth and Alexander's
## English Tea Room
*23808 Bothell / Everett Highway*
*Bothell, Washington 98021*
*425-489-9210*
*deanandsuehale@aol.com*

*From I-405, take exit #26. Turn toward Bothell and go 1 mile. The tea room is on the right. Look for the double deck red London bus next to the tearoom.*

Dean and Sue Hale patterned their tea room after those found in their son-in-laws hometown of East Bourne, England. Their brochure asks you to, "imagine a place where you unburden your cares and let time slip sideways". Such is the atmosphere at their tea room and gift shop. We were seated in the "Churchill" room which was done in a "hunting theme" with it's deep green and dark rose décor, accented with complimentary floral patterned table cloths and long white curtains on the windows. The other two rooms were equally attractive and interesting.

Once settled in, you select your tea from the variety offered under the Barnes and Watson label. Teatime offerings are the Cream Tea, Elizabeth's Tea, Alexander's Tea, and the full Afternoon Tea and they range in price from $5.95 to $17.95. Our tea choice was the Alexander's Tea, which was served plated in the most attractive manner and was priced at $9.95. Children's tea for those under 12 years of age, is offered for $6.95. Dietary needs will be accommodated with advance notice and groups are welcome. Breakfast and lunch are available daily and a wonderful 5 course English Dinner is offered on weekends.

MC/V/Checks          Wheelchair Accessible          Parking lot

*Mon-Sat: 8-4 - breakfast, lunch and afternoon tea. Tea times - 11 to 4 p.m. Reservations suggested 2 weeks in advance with a 1 wk cancellation policy. Fri & Sat: 6-9 p.m. English Dinners*

*Proprietor's*
*Autograph*_____*Date*_____

# The Enchanted Tea Garden

*3208 - 6th Street*
*Tacoma, Washington 98406*
*253-756-6603*

*Take I-5 to the Hwy 16 (Union) exit. Turn right and follow to 6th Avenue.*
*Take another right and the tea room is 3 1/2 blocks down on the right hand*
*side of the street.*

On our most recent visit to this tea room, even though it was late September, we were lucky enough to be seated in the "enchanted garden". We had it to ourselves so were able to really look for the many things that make it so special. Besides the many gnomes, frogs and bunnies that dot the garden, this appeared to be the final resting place for many teacups that had outgrown their usefulness due to broken "limbs" and cracked "lips"! Flowers, greenery and a stately old Russian Olive tree, as well as eclectic chairs and tables, add the final touches to this respite at the end of the walkway.

Inside the 100 year old bungalow, which has served as a tea room since 1998, tea tables are set amid shelves laden with several varieties of tea, gifts and tea necessities. Take time to look about before leaving the premises.

There are three tea sets to choose from starting with a Cream Tea of scone, fruit, jam and Devonshire cream at $6.00, followed by the Afternoon Tea which includes a sandwich, scone & jam and fruit garnish for $9.50 ($18.00 for 2). John and I select different sandwiches so we can have two varieties! The last selection is the Queens tea which consists of a sandwich, fruit and assortment of desserts, served on a tiered server for $16.95 ($29.95 for two). All include a pot of tea. The tea items can be purchased a la carte. Green salad (mixed greens and seasonal fruit tossed with ginger lime dressing), spinach salad and Greek salads are available for $4.25 to $9.00, depending on the size you choose. Special Theme teas may be arranged.

MC/V/AE/DIS/Checks    Wheelchair Accessible    Free Street Parking

*Open Monday through Friday 10-5, Saturday 11-5 and Sunday 12-3.*
*Tea time is 11-4 Monday through Saturday and Sunday 12-3. Reservations*
*are recommended but not necessary.*

*Proprietor's*
*Autograph*_____*Date*_____

# *Everything Tea*

*1015(B) First Street*
*Snohomish, Washington 98290*
*360-568-2267*

*Take Hwy 9 east to Snohomish Exit. Turn right on 2nd Street and right on Avenue D. The store is on the left side of the street.*

Chris and Patricia call their business, Everything Tea, "1200 square feet of Tea Lovers Paradise". How right they are! There are over 200 loose teas available in this shop as well as a very large selection of tea accessories. I even found something I didn't have!

The shop has moved into a more spacious building, which was formally an antiques shop, in order to expand their line of teas and to offer more of the "fun stuff", such as, tea pots, kettles, cups and saucers, cozies and lots of unusual and handy accessories (those spout doilies really do prevent the spout from leaking!).

There are far too many tea labels to list but some examples are Bewley's, McGrath's, Ahmad, Barry's, Jackson's of Piccadilly, Market Spice, Metropolitan Tea Co., and India Tea Co. Their house blend is Duncan's Ultimate Herbal Blend. As you can see, every kind of tea is represented and free tea sampling is available on Saturday and Sunday.

On one side of the room there is a cozy alcove with couches and tables where you may take time for a little conversation, or you may choose to pick up one of the magazines on the "tea" table and get in a little reading while you sip.

Whatever your reason for visiting Snohomish, be sure to take time to check out this very friendly business and catch up on the newest trends in teas.

MC/V     Wheelchair Accessible     Free Street Parking

*The shop is open 7 days a week, Monday through Thursday 10-6, Friday and Saturday 10-7 and Sunday 11-5.*

*Proprietor's*
*Autograph*_____*Date*_____

# The Exhibitors Mall & Trellis Café

*10312 - 120th Street E, # 4*
*Puyallup, Washington 98374*
*253-841-0769*
*mscampbell5@lycos.com*
*kimariejohnson@yahoo.com / exhibitors.mall.com*

*Take Hwy 512 to Eatonville exit. Follow*
*Meridian to 120th St. E, turn left, go one block.*
*The building is on the right hand side of the*
*street.*

The Exhibitors Mall was initially established as an art gallery with antiques. When Joe and Kimarie purchased the business in 1994, they intended to add a restaurant but first started expanding by inviting local artisans to show their wares. There are now 80+ cottage industries sharing space in the mall, along with major retail lines. Customers can shop from all the booths and check out one time!

The on site café is now managed by Shelley Campbell and has been named The Trellis Café. The menu offers soup, salad, sandwiches, dessert...and afternoon tea. The Afternoon Tea offers fancy finger sandwiches, fresh baked scones, decadent chocolates and seasonal fruit, all served on a tiered serving tray, complete with endless tea for $12.95.

Children's tea parties, which are $9.95 per person, are similar to Afternoon Tea but are scaled to fit the "little prince or princess".

I have always believed that antique stores are the perfect locale for a little tea room and here you will find just that. Shop a little, take a tea time break, and shop some more. Though we weren't able to stop here on a recent tea room tour, the Exhibitors Mall will definitely be on our schedule the next time we head north!

MC/V/DC/Checks          Wheelchair Accessible          Parking Lot

*Store hours-Mon. to Sat. 10-5, Tues. until 7. Café hours-Mon to Sat.*
*11-3:30, Tues. until 6:30. Afternoon Tea time is by reservations only.*

*Proprietor's*
*Autograph_____Date_____*

# The Fotheringham House

2128 W. Second Avenue
Spokane, Washington 99204
509-838-1891 fax 509-838-1891
innkeeper@fotheringham.net
www.fotheringham.net

*From I-90:*
*Eastbound, take exit 280; Westbound, take 280A,*
*turn north on Second Avenue. Turn left, stay in the*
*right lane to 2120 West Second Avenue.*

*From the Airport:*
*Follow the signs to Spokane. Take the West Spokane exit. This will take you*
*on a 4-lane highway and down a steep hill. Continue through the stop light*
*and across the bridge. Immediately at the end of the bridge, turn LEFT. Go*
*up the hill to Second Avenue. Turn right. It is one block to 2128 West*
*Second.*

Fotheringham House is the perfect example why I recommend to fellow teas enthusiasts, "check out a bed and breakfast when looking for tea". Many towns do not have a traditional Tea Room, but most small towns have bed and breakfast inns, and they may offer tea time. Those that don't have a set time, often will present a tea to a private group, if previous arrangements are made and the minimum number of guests can attend. You have nothing to lose by asking and everything to gain.

This 1891 Queen Anne-style house was built by David B. Fotheringham, the first mayor of the city of Spokane, as his family residence. The current owners/innkeepers, Paul and Irene, say, "fate brought us to the house". They kept clippings of the house on their refrigerator, never expecting to visit it. Then, they attended a party in Spokane and stayed at Fotheringham House. They loved the house, and the owner told them that it was for sale. That night they decided that they would be the next owners.

The house has all the details we expect when visiting a Victorian Mansion; a formal dining room, comfortable sitting rooms, a large wrap-around porch and a back yard with a fountain, birdbaths and arbors. All of those amenities are the perfect setting for afternoon tea. When taking tea at Fotheringham, you are treated to a step back in time, to when tea in the parlor was an every day event. Whether taking tea in the dining room, with it's cozy fireplace, floor to ceiling lace curtains and pastel and lace covered tables, or on the wicker bedecked veranda, you will enjoy a leisurely and traditional tea.

High Tea, which is $21.00 per person, consists of soup, salad, English tea sandwiches, scones, Devonshire cream, lemon curd, Strawberry jam, and four desserts. In the summer, when the weather is warmer, quiche or another entrée is served in the place of soup. Besides the weekly tea, Irene does theme and Christmas Teas, all with a Victorian influence.

For groups of 10 or more, a menu is available that includes breakfast and lunch fare. Total seating available is 28 people.

After a leisurely tea, do take time to walk about the beautiful grounds which boast thirty American climbing roses and sixty Old Garden roses, as well as, lavender hedges bordering the front walk. Lavender also share space with peonies and roses along the fence line. Peek into the gift shop where you can pick up a special memento of the day. Before you leave, visit the near-by Patsy Clark Mansion or perhaps take a stroll through the park, both of which are conveniently located across the street. Whatever your choice, take your time and take in the beauty of Fotheringham House.

MC/V/AE/Checks     Not Wheelchair Accessible     Street and Lot Parking

*Open all year except January. Tea time is Thursday from 11:30-2:00 and is open to the public. Reservations required by the night before. Parties of 10 may make reservations for any day.*

*Proprietor's*
*Autograph*_____*Date*_____

# *Hattie's Restaurant*

*51 Cowlitz Street West*
*Castle Rock, Washington 98611*
*360-274-7019*
*www.hatties-castlerock.com*

*From I-5 take exit 48 west into town on Huntington Avenue (approx. 1 1/2 miles). At Cowlitz Street turn left, travel 2 blocks and you will see the Restaurant on the left hand side of the street, across from True Value.*

Though we didn't have time to take tea, it was apparent to us, when we stopped by for a visit, that Hattie's is a fun and interesting place to visit, whether for tea time, breakfast, lunch or dinner. The owner, Linda, offers what she calls, "Uptown class...down home cooking" and that is just precisely what you will find! I heard from a reliable source that the portions are generous, tasty and nicely presented. From what we saw, that was an accurate description.

The atmosphere of the restaurant, ice cream parlor and Victorian "house" afford you the opportunity to choose your ambiance. The Victorian House, which is off the main dining room, boasts deep purplish wall paper, period furniture, touches of lace, and décor that represents the Victorian era. This is a very special room set aside especially for tea. The main dining room was delightful and was the setting for a small recreation of a country kitchen and parlor, complete with a fireplace, set up under one of the large paned windows. Hard to describe but delightful to see! True to the name, hats are everywhere, so if you feel a little underdressed you may be tempted to don one of them, just as the servers did.

The breakfast menu is extensive and now features their "national award" winning Almond Stuffed Orange Glazed French Toast! For lunch you may choose from soup, salads, deli sandwiches, wraps, stuffed pitas, fish and chips, burgers or a custom made baked potato. The signature chicken salad is one of the favorite offerings, whether served on a bed of lettuce or in a sandwich. Reservations are recommended for dinner and, again, the menu is extensive. If you plan to reserve for a group, Hattie's boasts the largest table in the Northwest at 16 feet 3 inches. It is a sight to behold!

Should tea time be your meal of choice, a special menu is prepared just for you. It consists of a scone, salad, a selection of small sandwiches, fruit, vegetables, cheese and sweets, plus a fragrant pot of tea, for $11.95 per person. This is just what I am looking for when seeking out the event called tea time! I so look forward to returning to Hattie's!

MC/V/AE/DC/DIS/Checks        Wheelchair Access
Free Lot and Street Parking

*Tea is by reservation only with a 48 hour notice required. There is a 24 hour cancellation policy. The restaurant hours are Monday through Saturday 8 am to 8 pm. Closed Sundays and most holidays.*

*Proprietor's*
*Autograph*_____*Date*_____

# Hattie's Tea Room

9504 - 271st Street N.W.
Stanwood, Washington 98292-8054
360-939-0437

*From I-5, take the Stanwood exit and head west, on Hwy 532 for about 5 miles. Past the railroad tracks, take 84th, then take a left on 271st. Hattie' is 4 blocks down on the left hand side of the street.*

Another tea tour and another delightful find! What a nice time we had visiting with Betty and finding out the history of her tea room. Opened in 2000, the tea room is named for her grandmother, and her grandmother would be quite at home there. A Victorian cottage, Hattie's has been taken back to the day when tea probably was served in it's parlor. The rooms, with their dusty mauve/lavender walls and burgundy accents, are filled with antiques and collectables from that era. Of course, the Irish in me took note of all the lace accents on the windows, tables and shelves. Tea accouterments, gifts and home décor items are available for purchase and are placed throughout the house for your browsing pleasures.

The afternoon tea, which we enjoyed, is priced at $7.95 and includes, three sandwiches (tuna, egg salad and cucumber on a wonderful selection of breads), orange scones with Devon cream, lemon curd and jam, a brownie, Bavarian cream tart, petite four and a wonderful selection of seasonal fruits (blackberries, grapes, strawberries, kiwi, star-fruit and blueberries). The attention to detail on the presentation is notable - fish shaped tuna sandwich, cucumber sandwich resembling a flower, butterfly shaped scone and a round, cut-out brownie. Since it was warm the day we were there, we opted to have the mango iced-tea and I would drink that again regardless of the weather! Good tea, delicious food and pleasant company; what more could one ask for!

Wheelchair Accessible                    Lot Parking

*The shop is open Mon-Friday 10-5  and Saturday 10-4. Tea is served from 10-4 daily. Groups are welcome with reservations. Teas are offered for children, holidays and special events. Throughout the year, etiquette classes are taught by Susan Springer .*

Proprietor's
Autograph_____Date_____

# The Ivy Tea Room
## at B.J.'s Corner Cottage
*30 S. E. 12<sup>th</sup> Street*
*College Place, Washington 99324*
*509-529-4752 / 877-326-2661*

*The tea room is located south of Highway 12 at the corner of Broadway and 12<sup>th</sup> street.*

Owner Pat Choisser has a mission. It is to provide guests with a tasty low-fat vegetarian or meat cuisine, to serve a variety of teas from around the world and to give personalized service in a relaxing enjoyable non-smoking atmosphere. This is accomplished in the Victorian Tea Room where guests are served the freshest ingredients on antique English bone china and offered an extensive list of fine teas to choose from.

High Tea is an elegant four course event which includes a fresh fruit plate, a salad with a variety of greens, vegetables and delicious dressings; assorted open-faced tea sandwiches and a Dessert Finale. The cost of this 1-2 hours of visual and appetizing dining pleasure is $15.50 per person.

Besides tea, Pat offers a four course dinner for a minimum of 12 people by advance reservations. Dinner is served after 4:00 pm and is accompanied by live music for $18.50 per person. Lunch time choices include a potato bar, a selection of sandwiches, soup, burritos, nachos, lasagna, quiche, pastries and desserts, as well as a veggie juice bar. There is something for everyone and special needs can be accommodated.

MC/V/Checks          Wheelchair Accessible          Lot and Street Parking

*Open Sunday through Friday 1-6, evenings by appointment. Tea is offered from 11-5 or by appointment. Reservations are required for HIGH TEA with 24 hours notice. Cancellation fee.*

*Proprietor's*
*Autograph*_____*Date*_____

# Just Pretend

612 Lawrence Street
Port Townsend, Washington 98368
360-385-0159
minishjr@olypen.com

*The tea house is three blocks from Victorian downtown. Directions will be given at the time the reservation is confirmed.*

The last time we visited Port Townsend we looked high and low for a tea room. As we drove the streets and walked the old town area, we kept commenting that this charming town could certainly use a tea room. How we wish we had known about Patricia and her dress-up tea!

Tea at Just Pretend promises to be an unforgettable experience because Patricia puts so much of herself into it. You gather in a lovely Victorian cottage where she invites you to "dress up" with vintage clothing, hats, gloves and accessories. Then, a proper tea is set out for you to enjoy at your leisure. There will be tea sandwiches, fresh fruit, assorted sweets, cake and of course, a hot pot of tea. If you wish, a personalized menu or special theme may be accommodated. An activity, based on the theme of the tea, is presented and each guest is given a party favor as a remembrance of the day.

This is an opportunity to create a memory you will cherish forever...close your eyes and Just Pretend. What a delightful way to spend the afternoon!

Checks/Cash          Not Wheelchair Accessible          Free Street Parking

*Tea is served from 2-4 pm at a private home. Reservations are required and there is a one week cancellation policy.*

*Proprietor's*
*Autograph*_____*Date*_____

# La Connor Flats - A Garden

*15920 Best Road*
*Mt. Vernon, Washington 98273*
*360-466-3190*

*From I-5 take exit 230. Follow Weston Hwy 20 for 5 miles to Best Road.*
*Turn left on Best Road and go 2 miles. La Connor flats will be on the right*
*hand side of the road.*

We were looking for another tea opportunity that turned out to be a dead end, but luckily our travels took us to the property next door that is home to La Connor Flats - a garden. This oasis in the country is really beautiful and the hostess, Marjorie, was most gracious. It must have surprised her to find two strangers knocking on her door in the late afternoon inquiring about her tea room. Actually, her tea room is a "retired" granary that has been converted into a most charming and cheerful room...perfect for tea. Refinished hardwood floors and rustic barn board walls, along with matching oak chairs and tables set with double white linens and fresh flowers greet you. The room is rich with light and a feeling of the outdoors, as it overlooks the beautiful garden.

The set tea is served on depression glass and Marjorie has over 200 cups and saucers in her collection, which she uses for teas. The set tea, which is served in three courses, consists of a fruit cup, hot scones and jam, a trio of sandwiches and assorted desserts for $11.00 plus gratuity. Other items may be substituted upon request.

In the summer months, tea is served outside on the porch or in the beautiful English Country Garden. At one end of the garden there is a large gazebo which is used extensively for weddings and other celebrations. The gardens are open and in bloom, March through October, and the carpet of color is always  changing. We found it enchanting when we visited during the month of September.

*The granary is open during April and serves soup/sandwich during the Tulip*
*Festival. Tea is by reservation, preferably at 2:00, throughout the year.*
*Small groups should give at least 24 hours notice. 8-10 people minimum.*

*Proprietor's*
*Autograph*_____*Date*_____

# *La La Land Chocolates*

*32279 Rainier Avenue*
*Port Gamble, Washington*
*360-297-4291*
*lalalandchocolates@yahoo.com*

*From downtown Seattle, take the Washington State Ferry Service to Bainbridge Island. Follow Hwy. 305 through Poulsbo to Hwy 3. Turn rt. (north) and continue to Port Gamble. Turn left at Gamble Bay. The nearest cross street is Hwy. 104.*

Janie started making her chocolates for holiday craft shows around 1996 and when the sales volume grew, she moved her business into a house in the historic town of Port Gamble. Customers commented that, "the sitting room would make a wonderful tea room" and the rest, as they say, is history. The tea room opened in 2002 and has developed a loyal following of very happy customers.

Since they were already serving scones, tea, coffee, cookies and fresh fruit with chocolate fondue, they incorporated a "Chocolate High Tea" into their offerings. For $14.95 per person, the tea includes a variety of tea sandwiches (smoked salmon, English cucumber with mint butter and Cotswold cheese with Roma tomatoes), cranberry pecan scones with home-made jam and clotted cream, orange blossom cookies, truffle of your choice, fresh fruit with chocolate fondue and a pot of loose leaf tea.

French press coffee or Mayan hot chocolate may be substituted as no extra cost. Chocolate truffles, fresh fruit & chocolate fondue, and, occasionally other pastries, are also available. Special dietary needs can be accommodated with prior arrangements.

Besides chocolates and high tea, tea tasting is presented once a month on a Saturday from 10-noon. The cost is $6.95 and reservations are required. Seating is limited so call early!

Checks/Cash          Not Wheelchair Accessible          Free Street Parking

*Open daily, except major holidays, from 9-5. Tea time is by appointment. Please call or email for reservations, at least the day before. Notice of cancellation is appreciated.*

*Proprietor's*
*Autograph*_____*Date*_____

# La Tea Da Teas

## at the Bradley House B and B

61 Main Street
Cathlamet, Washington 98612
360-795-3030b
radleyhouse@centurytel.net / www.bradleyhouse66.com

*Take I-5 to Long View and Long Beach to SR 4, which will bring you right into Cathlamet. From Astoria, cross the Astoria Bridge then turn right to SR 4 to Cathlamet. They are near the last ferry to Oregon!*

It just seems natural to me that a bed and breakfast would offer afternoon tea in the same tradition as the grand old hotels. So many B and B's are in turn of the century or early 1900's homes, with vintage furnishings and collections of memorabilia from the past...a fine setting for tea. Bradley House is just such a place. Built in 1907 as a gracious home of a lumber baron, this elegant home sits on a knoll overlooking the historic town of Cathlamet, Puget Sound and the mighty Columbia River. Tea is served in the dining room with it's expansive fireplace and large lace covered windows with floral valances. Shades of rose and pink give the room a soft, welcoming feel.

Audrian offers a large selection of themed teas from holiday to special occasion and each is custom made to suit your needs. A sample menu for High Tea might include chicken salad with grapes, jicama, green onions, slivered onions and parmesan cheese on Hawaiian bread, English cucumber marinated in Rice vinegar and sea salt on white bread with cream cheese, mini quiche, grain cracker with fresh brie and dried apricots, orange cranberry scones with lemon curd, raspberry jam and Devonshire cream. The selection of desserts could include petite four, mini cheesecake cube, cream puff, white chocolate macaroon and a selection of teas. All of this for $14.50 plus tax and gratuity. The tea menu varies and special needs may be accommodated. Lunch is available and reservations are recommended but not required.

Checks Accepted
No Wheelchair Access
Street and Lot Parking

*Open Monday through Saturday, 11-3. Tea is by reservation one week in advance. There is a 72 hour cancellation policy.*

*Proprietor's*
*Autograph*_____ *Date*_____

# *Madison's Tea Room*

## *at Between Friends*

*9111 State Street*
*Marysville, Washington 98220*
*360-658-9407*
*jennismith1@aol.com*

*From I-5, take 88th street exit. Go north on State Street 2.5 blocks. The tea room is on the left in green and white house. Watch for the "big clock tower" and the tea sign.*

When visiting Madison's, which opened in 2003, you may choose the setting that suits you because each of the three rooms offers a different ambiance. You may be in the mood for stepping into the past and choose the antiques filled room, or you may feel like a little whimsy that day and choose the mural clad garden room. Then, of course, the traditional Victorian room may be just what you are looking for.

When you find your niche, you must make a choice again, as there are numerous tea sets. The Cuppa Tea, with fruit and sweets is offered for $4.95 and if you add a scone, you have the Cream Tea for $7.95. The Afternoon Tea includes soup, a scone and sweets for $8.95, while the Duchess Tea adds salad and fruit to the precious tea for $9.95. The Garden Party offers green salad, two vegi-delight tea sandwiches, fruit and sweets for $10.95 and the low tea consists of scone, four assorted tea sandwiches, fruit and sweets for $12.95. The spectacular Victorian Tea has choice of soup or salad, scone, four assorted tea sandwiches, fruit and sweets for $14.95. Choice of tea is included in all the teas and scones are served with Devonshire cream, lemon curd and jam. For the children, Linda and Jenni have created Sweet Madison for children under 12. It includes a scone, two tea sandwiches, fruit, and tea room sweets. Ala carte items are available by request. They have a deli next door which offers soups, sandwiches and salads, as well as an espresso cart.

Before leaving, take time to check out the gift area which offers Harney and Sons tea, gifts, home décor, bath and body items and specialty foods.

MC/V/AE/Dis/Deb　　Wheelchair Accessible
Street and Lot Parking

*Tea time is Tuesday through Sunday 11-4. The gift shop is open until 6. Reservations are recommended a day or two ahead. If you must cancel, a call would be appreciated. Themed teas are offered during the holidays. Groups are welcome with reservations.*

*Proprietor's*
*Autograph*_____*Date*_____

# *Mc Gregor's Scottish Tea Rooms*

430 E. 25th Street.
Tacoma, Washington
253-272-4261
www.mcgregorstearoom.com

*Take the Tacoma Dome exit. The tea room is in a
row of shops across from the Tacoma Dome Station
in Freighthouse Square.*

My Robertson ancestors must have led me to this lovely Scottish tea room, and upon seeing it, I felt an immediate connection. Located behind the Tacoma Dome in a newly restored warehouse, there are rows of shops galore and eateries of every description. The tea room is at the very far left end of the building, across from an art gallery. There are a few tables set out in the common area but most are inside the tea room, which is reminiscent of a late 1800's Glasgow tea room.

The small cheery tables are covered with white linen table cloths, and there is an additional cloth, across the middle of each, in a beautiful burgundy and green McGregor tartan. Windows line the walls on the west side, and along with the ceiling treatment, create a light and comfortable setting.

The lunch menu offers meat pie or soup AND sandwich for $7.75. The meal includes oatcakes, cheese, fruit and dessert. Soup OR sandwich are available $4.95 and they are served with fruit, cheese and oatcake. All include a 2 cup pot of tea, coffee or hot chocolate.

There are three tea menu's available from the cream tea for $4.99 to the high tea for $14.95. High tea is served in a private dining room and is a meal in itself. It includes salad, meats, traditional baked specialties, fruit, oatcakes, cheeses and dessert. Beverage is included. For the lighter appetite there is an Afternoon Tea of tea sandwiches, scones and rolls, fruit, oatcakes, cheese and sweets for $8.95. If a soft drink is your drink of choice, they swerve Irn Bru, The #1 seller in the British Isles!

MC/V/Dis/AE/Checks     Wheelchair Accessible     Street Parking

*Open Tues.-Sat, 11-5 and luncheon is offered Tues-Sat., 12-2. Afternoon
Tea is offered Tues-Sat, 1-4. Tea time on Sundays is from 1-4. High Tea is
by reservation for groups of 6-12.*

*Proprietor's
Autograph*_____*Date*_____

# Mr. Spots Chai House
## Home of Morning Glory Chai
*5463 Leary Avenue N.W.*
*Seattle, Washington 98107*
*206-297-2424*
*info@chaihouse.com / www.chaihouse.com*

*From I-5, take the 50th Street exit, head west and take a left on Phinney Ave.*
*Then take a rt. on 46th which becomes Market St. and continue down the*
*hill. Take a left at Leary Avenue and the shop is on the rt. next to the park.*

This may not be what most of us think of as a tea room but they do offer
a very large selection of bulk teas. The owner, Jessica, refers to the décor as
"Gypsy Funk", which to me implies fun and a change of pace. As for teas,
they offer 45 single herbs, 35 blacks, green, 13 high grade oolong and
scented. The house tea is Morning Glory Chai. There is something for everyone's taste!

Besides tea, a selection of food items are available including pasties,
samosas, falafel, calzones, soups, grilled cheese sandwiches and bagels. If
dessert is what you are craving, cheese cake with chai and fancy cakes are
also on the menu. Beer and wine as well as an espresso bar round out the
beverage selections.

It seems like this could be the place to stop before heading to the Bay
Theatre, or perhaps a picnic at Bergen Place Park is in order. Whatever your
desire, this tea house offers a good selection of food and beverages to suit
everyone's taste.

There is a gift area on the premises offering bath items, imports, incense,
candles, and herbs. Bulk tea is also available for purchase.

MC/V/AE/Checks                                          Wheelchair Accessible
                     Metered and Free Street Parking

*Monday through Thursday 7 am -10 pm, Friday - 7 am - 11 pm, Saturday 8*
*am - 11 pm and Sunday 8 am to 8 pm. Anytime is tea time!*

*Proprietor's*
*Autograph*_____*Date*_____

# Mrs. Pennycooke's Tea Room

922 - 1st Street
Snohomish, Washington 98290
360-568-5045 / Website being developed

*Snohomish is located 30 minutes north of Seattle or 10
minutes east of Everett, off of State Route 9, which is easily
accessible from I-5 or Hwy 405. Snohomish is also 5 minutes west of Monroe, off of Hwy 2.*

I am beginning to think that tea rooms were put on this earth to test my
character, and Mrs. Pennycooke's, which opened in 2002, is just one of
those places. This lovely tea room, with it's soft 'Feathery Green and Divine
Blue' walls, sparkling white furniture and pale yellow plaid table cloths, is
also home to a very sizeable collection of Royal Family memorabilia. I heard
that both owners, Doris and Carole, are Royal Family collectors, just as we
are! The exclusive use of silver teapots, flatware, and cream & sugar sets
gives the room a rather regal touch.

Located in the heart of Historic Downtown Snohomish, which is known
as "The Antique Capital of the Northwest", this is the perfect place to stop
for a break from shopping, to enjoy a "cuppa" or a delicious tea set. For a
special event or if the company is special, request the charming "Alice
Room" which seats 2-4 people.

Light breakfast items are served from 10-11:30 Monday through Saturday. The Luncheon menu features attractively presented soups, salads and
sandwiches priced from $4.75 to $7.75. Tea offerings range from the Cuppa
Tea (tea and sweet) for $6.75 to Mrs. Pennycooke's Traditional Afternoon
Tea for $16.50. The latter includes an assortment of tea
sandwiches, cheese and fruit, scones with clotted cream,
jam, lemon curd, special sweets, cake of the day and pot
of tea of your choice. There is a Prince or Princess Tea
for $10.25. Desserts and scones are also available a la
carte. Mrs. Pennycooke's serves and wholesales their
own tea label.

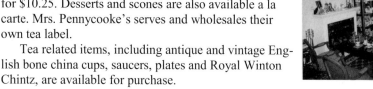

Tea related items, including antique and vintage English bone china cups, saucers, plates and Royal Winton
Chintz, are available for purchase.

MC/V/Checks          Wheelchair Accessible          Free Street Parking

Open Mon-Sat. 10-5 and Sun. 12-4. Tea is served Mon-Sat. 2-5 and Sun. 12
to 4. Reservations are recommended for parties of 5 or more though groups
are welcome if space is available. There is seating for 46 people.

*Proprietor's
Autograph*_____*Date*_____

# Peach Tree Bakery and Tea Garden

## In Country Village
*Bothell, Washington 98021*
*425-483-2005*
*crablad@foxinternet.com*

*From I-405, take exit 26 and drive south for 1 mile. They are the only tea room in Country Village and are located in the back left near the fountain.*

The problem with doing a tea room tour is that you can't try everything everywhere you go! Since we were visiting a number of tea rooms the day we were here, we limited ourselves to the signature peach scone...it was wonderful! Kristine, the owner of the bakery and a graduate of the prestigious Culinary Institute of America in New York, runs the bakery with the help of her delightful mom, Iva.

The buildings in the village are done in a rustic theme with shingled siding and roofs. Flowers abound everywhere and the tea room has a wonderful garden, with period lamp post, right near the village fountain. Inside, soft green walls and window toppers in shades of coral stripes and floral print welcome you. The bottom cloths on the tables match the toppers and are topped by pretty white cloths. An abundance of light from the windows, flower arrangements, and the use of pastels and white, make the room warm and inviting. We spent our time in the Sir Mumford Room which was set off with lace, wicker, greenery and a charming wall mural.

Kristine has a number of teas to choose from and they range in price from $5.95 for the Penwyth Tea to $19.95 for the Afternoon Garden Tea for Two. The Penwyth is a pot of tea with scone, the Anna Duchess of Bedford is the above with seasonal fruit and the Lord Bradford adds four tea sandwich. Sir Mumfords's Grand Afternoon Tea includes all of the above plus a grand assortment of tart cakes. All include English cream or butter and preserves and a pot of tea. Penelope's Tea for the "kids" is priced at $7.95. Dessert Teas may be arranged.

A wonderful selection of tea related items and other gifts are set out on tables and shelves and the walls hold a large number of other temptations, especially if you like plates. A bakers case is laden with a selection of scones and other desserts to purchase a la carte.

Just know that this is no quick stop! You will want to spend lots of time in the company of Sir Mumford and then, there is the rest of the village!

| MC/V/Checks | Wheelchair Accessible | Parking Lot |
|---|---|---|

*Regular hours are Tue. through Sat. 10-6, Sun. 11-5 and Mon. 10-4. They change seasonally so, call before going. Reservations are required for parties over 4.*

*Proprietor's*
*Autograph_____Date_____*

# The Perennial Tea Room

*1910 Post Alley*
*Seattle, Washington 98101*
*tealadies@perennialtearoom.com*

*Located at the north end of Pikes Market*

Finding Perennial Tea Room was easy! We just followed the sidewalk north to the end, until we saw the bright floral windsock and very colorful window boxes strategically placed on the brick building. Both were an indication of the friendly and welcoming atmosphere we were about to enter.

I will admit we were about to board a cruise ship and sitting still was a bit of a challenge, but some how we managed. The owner, Sue, engaged us in conversation and assisted us in choosing our tea from the extensive selection of 70 bulk teas, both English and Irish. They carry their own Perennial Tea Room label as well as Barnes and Watts. Once served, we sat back and enjoyed our surroundings while sipping on a wonderful, piping hot cup of tea.

Though we were anxious to get going, we did take time to look at the eclectic collection of gift items which were neatly placed on the many shelves that occupied the tea room. I was particularly interested in the selection of tea related books while daughter, Alicia, was fascinated by the art deco tea pots and tea cups. The gift choices were interesting and unlimited.

I would recommend that you take a bit more time to explore Pikes Market, which is a veritable hub of activity, but be sure to take a break and have a cuppa at Perennial Tea Room. You will enjoy both the tea and the visit with the owners.

There is limited on street parking as well as a pay parking garage. Customers receive a partial validation with a $20.00 purchase.

MC/V/DIS/AE/Checks/Debit                    Wheelchair Accessible

*Open daily from 10-5:30 and Sundays from 10-5*

*Proprietor's*
*Autograph*_____*Date*_____

92

# *Petals Garden Café*
## *at Cedarbrook Herb Farm*
*1345 S. Sequim Avenue*
*Sequim, Washington 98382*
*1-360-683-4541 / fax 360-681-2813*
*www.petalscafe.com*

*From Hwy. 101 west take the Sequim Ave. exit. Go south up the hill and the café is on the right through the big green gates.*

What a wonderful location for an afternoon tea...in the greenhouse at an herb farm! Bronwyn Salmon, the proprietor of this establishment, says that she offers "farmers market cuisine" - earthy, creative, simple food, grown locally and served with style. Petals has been voted the best gourmet restaurant in Sequim so, this is surely a trip worth making!

There is a full service restaurant on the grounds and the food is Australian Fare. Lunch selections are numerous and interesting including such English favorites as Ploughman's Lunch and Bangers 'N Mash. For dinner, entrees include pasta dishes, beef, lamb, pork and seafood. Appetizers, soups, salads and grand desserts also grace the menu.

Afternoon tea is a work of edible art. It starts with berry sorbet and shortbread, followed by a three-tiered server laden with sandwiches, cake, petite fours, crumpet, sausage roll, and fresh scone with cream and jam. All of this is accompanied by a tea of your choice for $15.95. For those wishing to try something different, the house tea is lavender. Coffee is also available.

MC/V/AE/DIS/Checks     Wheelchair Accessible     Parking Lot

*The café is open daily from 11-8*
*Tea is served daily from 2-4. Large groups by reservation.*
*Outside catering is available.*

*Proprietor's*
*Autograph_____Date_____*

93

# Piccadilly Circus

*1104 First Street*
*Snohomish, Washington 98290*
*360-568-8212 / piccadillycircus@yahoo.com*

*Go East from Everett on Hwy 2 and take the first Snohomish Exit*
*(Snohomish-Bickford Avenue) Go two miles to 1st street and turn left. The*
*tea room is two blocks down on the right.*

What fun it was to enter this store and find a very large selection of British food and wares. It was apparent that Geoffrey and Marian put a lot of thought into just what they were going to offer and the selection was wonderful! Whether looking for the perfect gift or something to add to your collection of china, crystal, linens or English memorabilia, chances are you won't leave empty handed.

In the back of the store, through the magical doorway, one enters the most charming room where breakfast, lunch, dinner and afternoon tea are served. The domed ceiling with it's cloud covering, and the walls with their Yorkshire Dales Murals, are complimented by the relaxing sound of running water. Breakfast, which is served from 8-10:30, offers a traditional English breakfast for $7.95. There are other selections as well. For lunch, one may choose from such English favorites as Welsh Rarebit, Ploughman's Lunch and Meat Pies to chicken dishes and sandwiches. Dinners are offered Thurs., Fri., and Sat. nights and their steaks have been voted "Best in the Northwest".  Since afternoon tea is my passion, I was happy to see that they offer a tea set, priced at $13.95, which includes scones, finger sandwiches, cake, pastries, confections, fruit, sorbet and tea. Scones and desserts are offered a la carte. There are too many menu choices to list here, so I recommend that you check out Piccadilly Circus yourself...more than once!

MC/V/AD/DIS/DC/Checks
Wheelchair Access

*Open Sunday through Wednesday 9-5 and Thursday through Saturday 9-8.*
*Tea time is 11-5. Reservations are recommended but not required.*

*Proprietor's*
*Autograph*_____*Date*_____

# *Pleasant Times Tea House*

*307 Third Street (P.O. Box 414)*
*Endicott, Washington 99125*
*509-657-3727*

*Endicott is two hours from the Tri-Cities, and hour and 15 minutes from Spokane, 45 minutes from Pullman and 20 minutes from Colfax.*

Originally established in 1991, Pleasant Times is now located in a charming, ten room house (circa 1905) in the little farming town of Endicott. It has been lovingly restored and decorated to be enjoyed by patrons from near and far.

Throughout the entire house are cheerful displays of old and new, carefully chosen treasures offered for sale. The Nursery is the setting for gifts for baby and The Bunkhouse displays gifts for men. Jean says she has "something for everyone in every price range!".

Now that you have shopped, it is time to take an afternoon tea break. If you are looking for something light, you may choose the Dessert of the Day which is served with tea or coffee for $5.95, or scones served with Devonshire cream, butter, jam, fruit and coffee or tea for $8.95. For a little heartier fare, the Light Lunch consists of Scones with Devonshire cream, fruit, coffee or tea and the dessert of the day for $11.95 or you may choose the Full Lunch, which includes the entrée of the day, served with salad or fruit, roll, coffee or tea and the dessert of the day for $14.95. High tea, which must be pre-arranged, is a traditional 5 course tea featuring scones, Devonshire cream, fresh fruit or fruit salad, tea sandwiches & savories, assorted desserts and a complimentary cordial and take home remembrance. The cost is $25.00 pp and it is usually offered on the 1st and 3rd Saturday. A Young Ladies Tea is available for $8.95 per person and it includes "dress-up" items and a short etiquette lesson before tea is served. Special theme teas are presented throughout the year and private evening dinners may be scheduled for groups of 8 or more. The above prices include gratuity and state sales tax.

V/MC

*Open every Wednesday through Saturday, 11-5, with the exception of holiday breaks and the beginning of January. Large group luncheons and high tea reservations are to be paid one week ahead. Groups of 4 or more are one check, please.*

*Proprietor's*
*Autograph*_____*Date*_____

# Pomeroy Carriage House Tea Room

*20902 N.E. Lucia Falls Road*
*Yacolt, Washington 98675*
*360-686-3537*
*Pomeroy@pacifier.com / www.pacifier.com/~pomeroy*

*The directions are extensive so they are being published on the next page.*

The POMEROY LIVING HISTORY FARM depicts 1920's farm life and has been owned by the same family since 1910. It is on the National Register of Historic Places. Activities for this historical farm center around the 2 story, 6 bedroom log house that is complete with it's original furnishings.

This is a fully operational farm, but special events are open to the public during the year. Special seasonal activities include a Spring Herb Festival and a Pumpkin Festival. The farm is open to the public on the first full weekend of each month, June through September. All donations in the Carriage House Tea Room help support the POMEROY LIVING HISTORY FARM, a non-profit public benefit museum.

The carriage house, where tea is served, is also the location of a charming British Gift Shop. Though tea is primarily served upstairs, handicapped seating may be arranged in the gift shop. There are four offerings in the tea room: Tea and Scones for $5.95, a Dessert Plate with fruit and tea for $6.50, a tea place, which includes tea, scones, assorted tea sandwiches, sweets of the day and soup or fruit for $9.50 and a Ploughman's Lunch for $9.50. In England, a ploughman's lunch referred to the bread and cheese that was taken into the fields for lunch. Later this became "pub lunch" and was served on a place with pickled onions or pickled eggs. Today you may choose a sweet or dill pickle, pickled onions or English pickles.

There is an extensive tea list, but if you prefer, a latte cappuccino or mocha may be purchased for $2.00. All gratuities are gratefully accepted as a donation to the POMEROY LIVING HISTORY FARM.

MC/V/DIS/Checks      Handicapped Accommodated      Parking Lot

*Hours of operation are Wednesday through Saturday 11:30 to 3:00. Tea is served during those hours. They do not take reservations and there is a minimum $5.50 charge.*

*Proprietor's*
*Autograph_____Date_____*

# *Directions to Pomeroy House*
# *Tea Room*

From the South - Take I-5 North to The Battle Ground exit (exit 9). Go straight ahead at the traffic light (you're on 10th Avenue also known as SR-502). Turn right at the traffic light at 219th. Follow that to Battle Ground, turn left at the traffic light between Safeway and Fred Meyer (also SR-503). Go north on SR 503 for 5 1/2 miles. Turn right onto NE Rock Creek Rd. Follow that for 4 1/2 miles (it eventually becomes Lucia Falls Rd). They are on the Right.

Alternate from the South - Take I-205 north to exit 32 and take Padden Parkway East to the second traffic light which is 117th Ave (also SR-503). Turn left and follow SR-503 North to Battle Ground. From Safeway in Battle Ground, continue north for 5 1/2 more miles to NE Rock Creek Rd. Turn right and follow that for 4 1/2 miles (it eventually becomes Lucia Falls Rd). They are on the left.

From the North - From I-5 take exit 14 and turn left. Go to 10th Avenue. Turn Right then turn left at the traffic light onto 219th. Follow that to Battle Ground. Turn left at the traffic light between Fred Meyer and Safeway (SR-503). Go north on SR-503 for 5 1/2 miles. Turn Right onto NE Rock Creek Rd. Follow that for 4 1/2 miles (it eventually becomes Lucia Falls Rd.) They are on the left.

# Queen Mary Tea Room
## and Restaurant
2912 N.E. 55th Street
Seattle, Washington 98105
206-527-2770

QueenMary@queenmarytearoom.com / www.ueenmarytearoom.com

*From I-5, take exit 169 (45th St.) toward Univ. of Wash. Pass UW, cross the overpass and follow the loop to the rt. at the bottom of the hill. Go 1/2 block, turn rt. on 25th. Proceed to 55th and turn right then go about 4 blocks.*

Established in 1988, Queen Mary's is an authentic English Tea Room serving breakfast, lunch and traditional formal afternoon tea. The tea room is dressed to the 9's with dark wood "ivy topped" wainscoting and floor to ceiling draperies in floral shades of deep green and burnt orange. Lace curtains and cream colored table linens, as well as silver teapots with flowers, give the room it's finishing touches.

Breakfasts, which range from $5.25 to $9.50, include Bangers & Mash or Smoked Salmon Quiche. The Lunch menu, which is extensive, also offers a variety of English favorites priced from $6.25 to $10.95.

Afternoon Tea, though, is what most of us are looking for and here you will find a delicious tea and attractive set. Priced at $21.95 per person, the tea starts with a trio of sorbets served in a champagne glass with a finger of shortbread on the side. This is followed by a tiered server laden with a generous trio of chicken almond, fresh cucumber and mint, and smoked salmon with cream cheese sandwiches as well as a miniature scone, crumpet, English muffin, thumbprint jam cookie, London sugar cookie, lemon curd tart, chocolate raspberry teacake, assorted fresh seasonal fruit, homemade whipped cream, jam, marmalade and a pot of tea. A separate pot of water is presented, since tea tends to get a little strong as it sits! Queen Mary herself would have been impressed! Dietary needs may be accommodated with prior notice. Seasonal and themed teas are offered during the year and groups are welcome.

The house tea is Queen Mary label and is available for purchase along with other special items in the gift area so, allow yourself time to look around.

MC/V/Checks          Wheelchair Accessible          Street Parking

*Open Wed through Sun 9-4. Anytime is teatime! Reservations are strongly recommended. There is a 24 hour cancellation policy. Seasonal or themed teas are offered during the year. Groups are welcome.*

*Proprietor's*
*Autograph*_____*Date*_____

# The Rose of Gig Harbor
## Bed & Breakfast - Tea Room
3202 Harborview Drive
Gig Harbor, Washington 98335
253-853-7990
rose@gigharborrose.com / www.gigharborrose.com

*From I-5, take the Hwy. 16 exit. Cross the Tacoma Narrows Bridge and take City Center Exit. Go right on Pioneer and left on Harborview. The tea room is near the City Pier.*

True to its' name, this tea room carries out the rose theme down to the Desert Rose dishes that grace the tables. Soft pink walls surround you and soft sheer curtains filter the sun into this very inviting get-away. Whether you "come for tea" or one of the many other offerings, serenity surrounds you.

Morton and Nancy offer a full luncheon menu of soup, salad and sandwiches, plus such specialty items as quiche or Cornish pastries.

If afternoon tea is what you are looking for, you'll find it here. The choices are scones and a pot of tea for $6.00; the Lady Rose tea which adds fruit for $8.00 and the High Tea which includes scones, fruit, sandwiches, an old fashioned dessert and a pot of tea for $17.00. All are served with Devonshire cream and jam. Coffee, lemonade, soft drinks and hot chocolate are also available. Special dietary needs can be accommodated with advance notice.

If you are enjoying the atmosphere and just don't want to leave, remember, this is a Bed and Breakfast, too! Have some extra time? Take a moment to check out the gift shop.

MC/V/AE/DC/Checks         No Wheelchair Access         Free Parking

*The shop is open 7 days a week from 11-4 and tea is served during those hours. Reservations are recommended on weekends. There is a $3.00 sharing charge. Catering available.*

*Proprietor's
Autograph*_____*Date*_____

# The Rose Room
## at the Rosalie Whyel Museum of Doll Art
*1116 - 108ᵗʰ Avenue N.E.*
*Bellevue, Washington 98004*
*425-455-1116 / 1800-440-Doll / fax 425-455-4793*
*dollart@dollart.com / www.dollart.com*

*I-405 to Bellevue. Take NE 8ᵗʰ St. West exit. Turn right on 108 th. Avenue.*
*The museum is two blocks further. Bellevue Square Mall is just 4 blocks*
*from the museum.*

The museum of Doll Art provides enjoyment to all ages and genders. They are internationally known and have received many awards including the prestigious "Jumeau Award for the Best Private Doll Museum in the World". This recognition was presented in Paris in 1994 and it is a 10 year award.

Besides being a premiere doll museum, the facility is available for dinners, weddings, luncheons and other private events. It is the perfect location for a catered tea, with it's elegant Victorian ambiance and collection of antique furnishings and dolls. Somehow dolls and tea parties just go together!

Three packages for children's teas parties have already been established; the "Birthday Party", the "English Tea Party" and the "Do-It-Yourself Party". The Museum works with a select list of caterers to provide the best teas and luncheons both for children and adults. For more information on reserving this beautiful building or any portion of it for your next tea, call or email the museum directly.

MC/V/AE/Checks          Free Parking          Wheelchair Accessible

**_Tea is by reservation_**. *The museum hours are Monday-Saturday 10-5,*
*Sunday 1-5. Closed New Years, Easter, July 4ᵗʰ, Thanksgiving and*
*Christmas.*

*Proprietor's*
*Autograph_____Date_____*

# *Sadie's Tea for All Seasons*

*2711 Meridian*
*Bellingham, Washington*
*360-223-6646*

*Coming from the south, take I-5 to the Merid-*
*ian Exit, turn left and go south on Meridian*
*approximately 1 mile. Sadie's is on the right hand side of the street. It is a*
*two story, light pink, Victorian building. The nearest cross street is Illinois.*

When looking for Sadie's, keep an eye out for the trellis and picket fence, or you could miss it the first time around! This charming Victorian, with it's turn of the century antique furnishings, is tucked away next to a large building so you may not see it coming. Does this sound like a personal experience?

With it's interesting lay-out and abundance of curtain clad windows, this lovely home is the perfect setting for tea. Arlene, who has owned the tea room for about a year, has done some extensive remodeling and after a grand re-opening, is making plans to extend her menu. The tea set choices will be expanded and will change monthly, the pastries will change weekly and the soup selections will change daily. Salads will be added to the repertoire. Some of items now being offered are the cream tea for $4.50, the afternoon tea, which consists of assorted sandwiches, lemon sorbet, currant scone, sweets and tea for $12.95, and High Tea, which offers soup, savory tart, finger sandwiches, sorbet, assorted cookies and pastries for $18.95. All of the above items are available a la carte. A light lunch of soup, scone, Devonshire cream and jam is available from 11-3 for $5.95.

There are hand made hats and boas for all to enjoy while having tea. Books on tea cups, tea pots, sterling silver, all with current prices, are available for those who would like to look up one of "grandma's" old pieces. Customers are encouraged to "read while they sip" and books on antiques will be added monthly.

MC/V/AE/DC/Checks          Wheelchair Accessible
Street and Lot Parking

*Open Monday through Saturday 11-5. Anytime is tea time! Reservations*
*required 24 hours ahead for High Tea and for parties of more than 6. No*
*refund if cancellation is less than 24 hours.*

*Proprietor's*
*Autograph_____Date_____*

# Sassy Teahouse and Boutique

*16244 Cleveland Street*
*Redmond, Washington 98052*
*425-458-4988*
*Kathleen@sassyhouse.com*
*www.sassyhousecom*

*SR 520 East to Redmond Way exit. Go left, stay in left lane and turn left into Windermere parking lot after crossing Leary Way. The teahouse shares that lot. Town center clock is nearby.*

Kathleen has opened what she calls "a gathering place for friends big and small". Located in Redmond's historic 1814 Stone House, this charming cottage style tea house offers a shop where you can purchase a gift for a friend or a decorative accessory for your own home. Afterwards, relax in a comfy chair and enjoy a beverage from the espresso bar or a hot cup of tea. You can stay for lunch or tea, but if time is an issue, opt for take-out!

There is a nice assortment of hearty sandwiches at $6.95 as well as tea sandwiches at $5.95. Both include a side of salad or fruit. Entrée salads, baked goods and desserts are also offered.

Sassy Tea Decadence includes tea and a three tiered tower of sandwiches, scones, sweet cream & jam, and a variety of decadent petite tarts and sweets for $12.95. The Little Sassy Tea, for children 3 and up, consists of warm Sweet Vanilla Cream Tea or Teas 'R Us organic fruit tea, tea sandwich fingers, fruit and mini pastry for $4.95. There is even a children's corner designed for their littlest friends!

No wheelchair access due to Historic designation.
MC/V/DC/DIS/Checks                    Lot or Street Parking

*Monday to Friday 7 to 5, Saturday 9 to 5 and Sunday 10 to 5. There are no formal tea times. Reservations required for parties of 6 or more. Catering is available. 6 or more.*

*Proprietor's*
*Autograph_____Date_____*

# *Scottish Tea Shop Ltd.*

*1121 - 34th Avenue*
*Seattle, Washington 98122*
*206-324-6034*

*From I-5, take exit 200 and head east. Follow to State Avenue and turn right then follow to 76th St. (light) and turn left. The tea room is 1/2 block down on the left hand side next to Van Dam Flooring.*

Being a "card carrying" Dohachaidh, it was only natural that I should spend some time getting familiar with the Scottish Tea Shop. I probably spent more time checking out the gift area than looking at the tea offerings because there were so many products of Scotland that I hadn't seen before in this area. From the books and tapes to the beautiful crystal and china, everything was of the finest quality and genuinely Scottish.

Our visit with Jackie, who has owned the tea shop for seven years, was both interesting and educational, as she shared the history of tea in Scotland as well as her tea shop. Very much a neighborhood place, her customers are numerous and loyal, yearning for a place where they can sit for two to four hours visiting with friends and doing a little shopping, while enjoying afternoon tea with Scottish "hook". Small green tables set with genuine Scottish placemats, complimented by "comfy" soft chairs, seat up to 10 people. For a more intimate setting, green wing-backed chairs sit face to face by a lace covered back window. The tea set consists of cucumber with cream cheese, smoked turkey with Scottish chutney, Northwest smoked salmon and Virginia ham with Scottish mustard sandwiches, Scottish Oat Raisin Scone, Fruit and cheese with Scottish oatcakes, and Orkney Broonie with sticky toffee pudding sauce topped with ice cream, Scottish Shortbread, Scottish fudge and Scottish Tea Time Tea for $12.00 per person. Items may be purchased a la carte and there is a favorite menu choice of fruit, cheese and oatcake plate. Though we didn't take tea, we did get to taste the dark and flavorful Scottish scone!!

Not Wheelchair Accessible                    Street Parking

*Open Tuesday through Saturday, 10-5. Tea and lunch by reservation. There is no tipping for the tea!*

*Proprietor's*
*Autograph*_____*Date*_____

# The Secret Garden Tea Room

4041 Factoria Mall
Bellevue, Washington 98006
425-746-4557
secretgardentearoom@msn.com

*From I-405, take exit 10 ( Coal Creek Pkwy). At the end of the ramp, go east and follow the signs to Factoria Mall. They are located in the mall.*

Opened in 2003 by Wendy and Elizabeth, this tea room is conveniently located inside a mall. The shop is quite charming, with it's floral and lace draperies, white linen table covers and floral accents. The décor is English cottage, which makes one feel comfortable and welcome.

The tea sets include the Duchess Tea which is scones with Devonshire cream, jam and lemon curd for $6.95 and is only available before 11 and after 2:30. The Princess Tea is $17.95 per person and offers assorted tea sandwiches, savory bites, fresh fruit, plated sweets and scones with Devonshire cream, jam and lemon curd. The Queen Tea is $19.95 and it adds a cup of soup and orzo pea salad to the previous tea. The final tea set is the Ladies Afternoon Tea and it is only available after 2:30. With that tea you receive assorted tea sandwiches, fresh fruit, petite dessert plate and scones with Devonshire cream, jam and lemon curd for $12.95. All of the above teas include a pot of tea. For children under 6, Secret Garden offers a Teddy Bear Tea for $6.95, which has peanut butter & honey and cheese tea sandwiches, orange slice, grapes, scone with Devonshire cream, jam and lemon curd, teddy bear cookies and lemonade or tea. A slightly larger children's tea is the Tinkerbell Tea, which adds a sliver of quiche, fruit , cheese wand, and assorted sweets for $9.95. Inquire about their party packages.

Besides tea, luncheon items of soups, salads, sandwiches, quiche and petite desserts are offered. Their special is the Secret Garden Sampler which includes half a sandwich, cup of soup, orzo pea salad and frosty cranberry salad for $9.95. There is a minimum charge of $5.95 per person.

MC/V/AE/DIS/Checks          Wheelchair Accessible          Lot Parking

*Open Tuesday-Saturday, 10-4 and Sunday, 11-4. Anytime is tea time. Reservations are recommended but walk-in's are welcome if space allows. Some days, reservations are accepted and cancellations would be appreciate.*

*Proprietor's*
*Autograph*_____*Date*_____

# *Victorian Rose Tea Room*

1130 *Bethel Avenue*
*Port Orchard, Washington* 98366
360-876-5695
*admin@springhousegifts.com /www.springhousegifts.com*

*From State Route 16, take the Tremont exit. From the North, follow the exit.*
*From the South, take a right. Go straight until you reach the stoplight at*
*Bethel Rd. Take a left and go straight until you see Village Square, which is*
*located across from the Post Office. The tea room is the pink and blue build-*
*ing on the left.*

Victorian Rose Tea Room is in a charming "Painted Lady" style shop complete with a turret dining room. Groups of 10-24 may reserve the private upstairs room but there is no elevator. Larger group of up to 65 people can have full use of the downstairs dining room when pre-arranged, except between the busy hours of 12-2.

The breakfast menu offers Quiche, Eggs Benedict, Crepes, and other specialties for $3.95 to 6.95. Lunch and dinner are also offered, and you can contact the owner, Sandy, for details.

The tea menu offers a High Tea, which is usually served at 3:00, for $9.95 and it includes scones with whipped butter & jams, select fruit or veggies with dip, specialty desserts and tea or coffee. The Victorian Rose High Tea menu offers all of the above plus petite quiche and assorted tea sandwiches for $13.95. The prices do not include tax and gratuity and pre-paid reservations are *required.* If you are hosting a party and would like your guests to leave with a special memento, Sandy will set out her Fancy Floral Tea Cups, and each guest may take one home for an additional $8.00. Parties for children may be arranged for $ 6.95 per person.

A lovely gift shop, Springtime Dolls and Gifts, adjoins the tea room. It features many popular collectables as well as tea pots and tea sets.

MC/V/ DIS, checks          Wheelchair Accessible          Parking Lot

*The shop is open Mon. through Sat. from 9-7 and Sun. from 9-5. Breakfast,*
*lunch and dinner are served every day. Tea and desserts are available daily.*
*High teas are offered on select days of the month. Check their website for*
*specifics.*

*Proprietor's*
*Autograph_____Date_____*

# *Victorian Tea Connection*

*108 Vista Way*
*Kennewick, Washington 99336*
*509-783-3618*
*viconn@urx.com / www.victorianconnectiongifts.com*

*Hwy 395 north from Umatilla, take a right turn on Vista Way. From the south take a left on Vista Way. Clearwater joins into Vista Way. The nearest cross street is 395 and Clearwater.*

Isolyn and Simon refer to their tea business as a "mom and pop kind of shop", where the needs of the customer are a priority to them. The tea area is inside their gift store in an area where the tea patrons will not be disturbed.

There is one afternoon tea offered at a cost of $10.00 and it consists of scones with Devonshire cream and preserves, 3 or 4 different tea sand-wiches, savories, fruit and pastries, and your choice of fine Ashby's Tea. They continually fill your tea pot with boiling water to keep the tea hot! Each guest is given a choice of tea flavor, and they have many to choose from including, decaffeinated and herbal infusions.

The gift shop, which encompasses 1800 square feet, carries a large line of Ashby's tea as well as a variety of preserves and curds from England. They also carry fine china and crystal, lamps, linens and lace, framed artwork, collectables and much more. If there is something you are looking for but do not see in the gift shop, Isolyn will be more than happy to track it down for you. The emphasis is on service at Victorian Connection.

MV/V/AE/Checks          Not Wheelchair Accessible          Parking Lot

*Hours of operation are 10-6 Monday through Saturday. Tea time is 3:30-6. Reservations are required; 2-6 people 3 days and 7-12 people 1 week. No refund will be offered if reservation is cancelled.*

*Proprietor's*
*Autograph_____Date_____*

# The Victorian Tea Garden

*614 The Parkway*
*Richland, Washington 99352*
*509-946-3606*

*The nearest cross streets are George Washington Way and Lee Blvd.*

The owner, Lisa, describes her tea room as "Victorian with British food" The menu certainly lives up to that description! Luncheon is served from 11am and includes English Meat Pie and Brocato Pie for $7.95 and sandwich choices such as egg/olive, cheese pimento or chicken salad, with fruit, cheese, crackers, a cup of soup and dessert also for $7.95. A cup of soup of the Day served with fruit, cheese and crackers is $3.95.

Four scones or a crumpet with fruit and your choice of butter, Devon cream, jam or lemon curd is $5.95. Afternoon tea is available for $9.95 and it includes a variety of teas with savories and sweets, delicate tea sandwiches, fruit, crackers and cheese.

Lisa asks that you, "please take time to enjoy a leisurely afternoon tea, as it is never a hurry at The Victorian Tea Garden".

MC/V/AE/DIS/DC/Checks     Wheelchair Accessible
Street & Lot Parking

*Open Mon. 10:30-2 and Tues. through Sat. 10:30-4. Tea times are Mon. 12:30-2 and Tues. through Sat. 1-4. Reservations are required for groups of 6 or more for Afternoon Tea as well as High Tea from 5:30-7.*

*Proprietor's*
*Autograph_____Date_____*

# *Vintage Inn B & B*
## *& Tea Parlor*
*310 W. 11th Street*
*Vancouver, Washington 98660*
*360-693-6635 or 888-693-6635*
*info@vintage-inn.com / www.vintage-inn.com*

*From I-5 take exit 1-C. Go west on 15th St. and turn left at W. Columbia Street. Go four blocks to 11th Street and turn right. The Inn is on the left hand side in the middle of the block.*

Situated in the heart of the antique district, this 1903 Victorian Inn has it all...great hospitality, a wonderful place to stay and afternoon tea. What more could one ask for? Furnished in elegant antiques, seating for tea is in the formal dining room and garden room.

During our stay at Vintage Inn, we took advantage of the opportunity to experience the full 5 course afternoon tea. Doris prepares everything on site and custom made for each group. Our offerings consisted of date walnut scones, watermelon soup, assorted sandwiches, fruit kabobs, a very attractive selection of specialty desserts, and bottomless pots of teas. This was a most generous tea at $16.95 plus tax per person.

The table was set with antique china, crystal glasses and linen luncheon napkins. Fresh flowers from the garden adorned the table and our plates, and home grown herbs were used in the recipes as well as to garnish the dishes. Everything was delicious and presented in such a beautiful manner. The motto of the tea parlor is, "Tea Urges Tranquility of the Soul", and it certainly did for us.

Specific dietary needs can be accommodated with prior arrangements. There is a small gift area of specialty tea items to tempt you before you leave this wonderful piece of heaven!

MC/V/Checks                    Street Parking and Small Lot

*Teas are any day or time by appointment. Reservations are required at least 1 week in advance. 2 day cancellation policy. The minimum reservation is 6 people and maximum is 24.*

*Proprietor's*
*Autograph_____Date_____*

# Wild Sage
## World Teas, Tonics & Herbs

227 Adams Street
Port Townsend, Wshington 98368
360-379-1222
wildsage@olypen.com
www.wildsageteas.com

*Just off the main street (Water Street ) on Adams.*

The world of tea is waiting to be discovered in this cozy, unique teahouse in downtown Port Townsend. Featuring a wide assortment of more that 100 teas from around the world, Wild Sage is often quoted as saying, "so many teas, so little time". Specializing in fine black tea blends from England (Taylors of Harrogate), exquisite loose-leaf white, green and oolong teas (Tao of Tea), wonderful black and green blends (Harney and Sons) and exotic herbals from around the world, Wild Sage carries all types of fine teas in bulk, loose leaf tin, as well as tea bags. The tea house promotes and encourages the discovery of tea, it's ancient culture, the life style and tea's many health benefits.

Wild Sage serves over 40 teas in bulk, either by the cup or by the ounce and encourages customers to "try before they buy". Staff delights in providing customers with tea information and answers to their personal tea questions.

This creative teahouse provides a serene retreat from the busy world. In addition to the teas, tonics and herbs served, Wild Sage serves delicious, local baked goodies, Belgian chocolates and Elixir Chinese health tonics. They specialize in 6 different types of masala chai's, fine high mountain oolongs, excellent China greens or robust breakfast blends, and herbals from around the world.

Many customers are drawn to the store simply by it's natural, enticing aroma. So, next time you are in Port Townsend, Washington's Victorian seaport, amble into Wild Sage teahouse and re-discover the wonderful world of teas, tonics and herbs waiting for you.

There is a gift shop featuring tea accessories, tea pots and gifts, for your browsing pleasure.

MC/V                                          Wheelchair Accessible

*Store hours are Monday through Saturday, 10-5:30 and Sunday, 11-5:30. closed Tuesdays.  Anytime is tea time!*

*Proprietor's*
*Autograph*_____*Date*_____

# *Your Cup of Tea*

*425-334-9751*
*Fax 360-658-8887*
*sspringer@att.net*

*Location is determined at time of booking*

Susan Springer is a trained and certified Tea Etiquette Consultant and is the founder and director of Your Cup of Tea, a company specializing in teaching tea etiquette for social and business occasions for adults and children in an entertaining, fun and enjoyable manner. Susan says that, "afternoon tea not only serves as a social function, but a professional one as well and can be an alternative to the business luncheon or dinner".

Classes begin with a historical overview of the tea trade from its origin in China through the Victorian era and our present day tea rituals. Antique and unusual tea time accessories are demonstrated, as well as accurate information on the proper steeping techniques for a variety of teas and tisanes. Participants can meet in a tea room, have a private catered affair or simply invite Ms. Springer as a speaker for a workshop or special event. Ms. Springer has a Bachelor of Arts degree in Home Economics and is Certified in Family & Consumer Sciences. She is a member of the Specialty Tea Institute and is a graduate of the Protocol School of Washington, DC, the leader in etiquette and protocol services. A published author, she is a columnist for The Country Register newspaper and has written articles for Teatime Gazette, Tea A Magazine and Tea Room Guide and Digest.

If you need assistance planning your next tea event, are looking for an interesting speaker for your workshop or retreat or want to present a class to adults or children on proper tea etiquette, contact Ms. Springer to make arrangements.

*Susan is a consultant and is available by appointment.*

*Proprietor's*
*Autograph*_____*Date*_____

*Welcome*

*to*

*British*

*Columbia*

# *Applewood Country Gifts*

## *Gifts, Tea Room, Bakery and Fudge*
*#112 - 6345, 120th Street*
*North Delta, B.C., Canada V4E 2A6 / 604-596-9007*

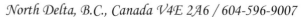

*Take Hwy 99 to Hwy 10 exit. Proceed to Scott Road (120th Street) then go north to 64th Avenue. They are located on the SW corner of Scott and 64th in "Sunshine Village" tucked behind 7-11.*

Sometimes we feel especially lucky in our search for tea rooms around the Northwest. When you have the opportunity to meet people as nice as Carol and Marianne, you know it is one of those days! If another tea room proprietor hadn't told us about Applewood, we would never have had the opportunity to meet these gracious and friendly "grandma's".

They have been in business for 10 years and have been offering tea for the last six years. The tea room area of the shop is fun and welcoming. The soft yellow wallpaper, with tea cups scatter all over it, fresh flowers on the tables and the "aprons" valance with lace bottom curtains, just invite you to take tea. EVERYTHING is mismatched...the tablecloths, chairs, tables, china cups and saucers, cloth napkins, plates, creamers, even other wall coverings! It is charming and very interesting!

Traditional High Tea is $15.00 CND and offer sandwiches, savories, scones and sweets. All of the items are available a la carte, as well. There is a wonderful children's tea party room set apart from the rest of the shop where children can enjoy a supervised tea for $12.50 CND per child with clothes for dress-up, party table games, goodie bags and more. A special cake may be purchased separately.

Lunch items such as quiche, shepherds pie, and grilled focaccia sandwiches as well as soup and baked goods, like their famous rhubard upside-down cake, are also available. This is a bakery and fudge shop, and if you need to put your sweet tooth on hold, just purchase one of the delicious baked goodies of some of their signature fudge to take home. Don't forget to check out the large gift area with it's vintage and contemporary items.

MC/V/DEB/Checks          Wheelchair Accessible          Parking Lot

*Open Monday through Saturday, 10-5:30. Reservations are not required but are advisable, especially for large groups.*

*Proprietor's*
*Autograph*_____*Date*_____

# Bacchus Restaurant
## at the Wedgewood Hotel

*845 Hornby Street*
*Vancouver, B.C., Canada V6Z 1V1*
*604-608-5319*
*Bacchus@WedgewoodHotel.com / www.WedgewoodHotel.com*

*#1 Oak Street to 16th, left on 16th (west) to Hemlock, right on Hemlock onto Granville Bridge. Go to Smithe and turn left. Go to Hornby then take a right. The hotel is across from Lake Courts.*

What could be a better setting for tea than a grand hotel? With it's elegant old world European décor, the lobby of the Wedgewood offers the perfect background for afternoon tea. The dark wood, heavy drapery, plush upholstery and abundance of fresh flowers bring back the feel of a time when Queen Victoria herself might have stopped in for afternoon tea.

Owner Eleni offers a tea time that is rich with tradition yet suited to today's tastes. The tea plate consists of gourmet finger sandwiches, freshly baked scones with Devonshire cream and preserves, chocolate éclair, mini Bakewell tart, seasonal fruit tartlet and lemon cake with Swiss meringue at a cost of $21.00 CND. All of the above is served along with a Kit Royal or a glass of Moet Champagne for $36.00 CND. The tea list is lengthy and includes black, green, whole fruit tisanes and herbal infusions. Coffee is available and special dietary needs can be accommodated with advance request.

The award winning restaurant also offers Sunday Brunch and romantic dinners, so if you are staying in town, you might want to put one of these meals on your agenda. It's just another reason to savor the atmosphere a little longer.

MC/V/AE/DC        Wheelchair Accessible        Metered Street Parking

*The restaurant opens at 6:30am Monday through Friday and at 7:00am on Saturday and Sunday. Tea time is on Saturday and Sunday from 2-4. Reservations are recommended and there is a 24 hour cancellation policy. Groups are welcome but there is a minimum and maximum. Call for details.*

*Proprietor's*
*Autograph_____Date_____*

# The Blethering Place

*2250 Oak Bay Avenue*
*Victoria, B.C., Canada V8R 1G5*
*250-598-1413*
*tearoom@thebletherngplace.com*
*www.blethering.com*

*Highway #17 takes you into Oak Bay. The tea room is on the main thorough-fare, at the corner of Oak Bay and Monterey.*

This was the first tea room we visited in Canada many years ago. Though we weren't doing tea tours up until a few years ago, we always visited this special British tea room. Built in 1912 as a grocery store and post office, Blethering Place went through a few transitions before it finally became a tea room in 1975. Ken, the current owner, has built his business into a Victorian landmark enjoyed by locals and visitors alike. The emphasis is on friendly service and food that is "baked in their ovens"!

There are two tea sets, the first being Afternoon Tea, which is offered for $14.95 CDN. It consists of crust-less petite sandwiches, warm tea scones, Devonshire cream, fresh fruit, cake, sausage roll, butter tart, tea or coffee and Blethering Place strawberry jam. The Full Afternoon Tea, which is priced at $16.95 CDN, is the same as the above but it includes English fruit Trifle (a weakness of mine!). Scones, tea biscuits, cinnamon buns, Nanaimo bars and lemon or butter tarts may be purchased a la carte. Numerous beverages are also available.

If you are interested in heavier fare, other meals are available. For breakfast, interesting items that may tempt you are, Bacon Butty, Eggs Benny and Boiled Eggs and Soldiers, as well as traditional favorites like Belgium waffles, pancake and omelets. There is a lunch menu which includes soup, sandwiches, salads, quiche, and an extensive dinner menu offering roast beef, salmon, turkey dinner, leg of lamb, fruit and vegetable curry, bangers 'n mash, Shepherds pie, crepes and so much more! Many choices...delicious food!

After your meal, allow yourself time to check out the gift shop on your way out.

MC/V/DEB/Travelers Checks          Lot and 2 hr. Street Parking

*The shop is open Monday through Friday 8am - 9pm. Tea time is 11-7. Reservations are not required but are recommended.*

*Proprietor's*
*Autograph*_____ *Date*_____

# Butchart Gardens

P.O.Box 4010
Victoria, B.C., Canada V8X 3X4
250-652-4422 / 800-652-4422
email@butchartgardens.com / www.butchartgardens.com

*The address for the gardens is 800 Benvenuto Drive, Brentwood Bay*

It seems that everyone who visits Victoria makes Butchart Gardens a destination. We certainly do and we have found the perfect way to see the gardens twice...take a tea break!

Tea is served in the original family residence which is located on the grounds, and which everyone probably takes the time to see from the outside. The ponds and plants that surround the house are spectacular but the view from inside is just as breathtaking. Just knowing that this was the home of the founders of Butchart Gardens is magic in itself so, as the original residents surely did, take a few moments to enjoy afternoon tea in one of the beautifully appointed rooms with a view of the gardens.

There are two tea sets to choose from. The first is Afternoon Tea and that consists of a fruit cup with yogurt citrus dressing, savory tea sandwiches which include: egg salad and watercress, smoked salmon with caper berry mayo, cucumber & lemon pepper cream cheese, curried chicken mousse roll and an individual quiche, a selection of sweets which include: a chocolate flower pot, lemon poppyseed loaf, chocolate brandy Napoleon slice, shortbread cookie, a fresh fruit tart and candied ginger scone with berry jam and whipped vanilla Devon cream The cost of the tea is $21.00 CND. High Tea, which is $28.00 CND, includes an individual quiche, Cornish pastry with green tomato relish and Dijon mustard, the tea sandwich and dessert selections as described above, as well as a warm fruit turnover and toasted crumpet with melted butter and honey. Both are presented on tiered servers and include coffee or tea. What better way to take a break before venturing out into the gardens a second time!

MC/V/AE/DC        Wheelchair Accessible        Parking Lot

*The gardens are open every day, thought closing time varies depending on the season. Tea is offered from noon to 4 and reservations are recommended during the summer. Special dietary needs can be accommodated.*

Proprietor's
Autograph_____Date_____

# Chocolate Cottage

## and Truffles Tea Garden

1488 Old Yale Road
Langley, B.C., Canada
604-533-7611
info@chocolatecottage.com / www.chocolatecottage.com

*Take exit 66 and head south on 232nd. At the T junction, go left on Glover Rd. At the next intersection (Esso station), take a left onto 216th. Pass 56th Ave. then Fraser Hwy and go to the third intersection, which is 5 corners. There are two possible rights, take the immediate right onto Ole Yale Rd and they are 5 bldg. Down on the left.*

It is always special to find a new tea room on one of our tours, especially one as lovely as Truffles Tea Garden at the Chocolate Cottage. The former carriage house is now home to a chocolate factory and a tea room.

In the tea room, the rich golden yellow walls and blue décor, with touches of deep pink in the "ribbon" valances, just attacks the senses. Surrounded by lace adorned windows, the tables are covered in a deep blue with lace overlay and sit upon a cobblestone floor. The matching chair seats and backs are a woven design and the wood is natural oak. The rooms Tudor style trim was made from the buildings original wood. It is a room you have to see to appreciate!

Shirley offers three tea sets starting with the Hansom Cab Tea, which offers two scones and tea for $6.95 CND. The next offering is The Carriage Tea for $9.95 CND and it includes two scones, two tea sandwiches (cucumber/cream cheese and Watercress/tomato) and tea. High Tea is $20.00 CND and includes 4 tea sandwiches, scone, chocolate cup filled with fresh fruit, slice of lemon poppyseed cake, a Cottage truffle and tea. All of the above also include strawberry jam and Devon Cream. A Farrier's lunch of 1/2 sandwich and bowl of soup is offered for $9.50 CND.

Allow yourself plenty of time after tea to "wander down the cobblestone pathway" to a very special village where you might see Mr. T Crumpet, Mr. T Fish, Mr. H Cutter or Mr. Halli Butt. Of course, you might need to pay a call on Miss Primpher or Mr. Pot-tee! The Chocolate factory sits adjacent to the "village" and is a glassed-in wonder. You are welcome to stop and watch awhile! Don't forget to pick up some of their luscious chocolate to take home.

MC/V/Interact          Wheelchair Accessible          Parking Lot

*The chocolate shop is open 9-5 daily. Tea is served Mon-Sat from 10-4 and Sun from noon-4. Groups of up to 24 are welcome. Reservations are required for high tea.*

*Proprietor's Autograph_____ Date_____*

# Clancy's Tea Cosy

*15223 Pacific Avenue*
*White Rock, B.C., Canada V4B 1P8*
*604-541-9010*

*From south take 99 to White Rock exit ( Marine Drive/8th Ave). Proceed to*
*Stayte Rd. and turn right then turn left on Pacific. From the north, take Hwy*
*10 and turn right on Johnson. Follow Johnson to Pacific and turn left.*

It was such a treat to find this pleasant tea room in the heart of this charming ocean-side town. After driving down to the Promenade and doing a walk-about, we were ready to sit a while and enjoy a leisurely tea. The atmosphere is quite relaxing with it's almost garden like feel and Celtic music in the background. Burnt orange walls, with a deep green accent, are off-set with lots of lush plants, lace topped tables and interesting wall décor. Besides the large main room, which has a bank of windows facing the street, there is a cozy nook off to one side for a more intimate setting. Wherever you choose to sit, the service is friendly and prompt.

The owner is Dina and her partner is her mom, Willy. Then there are the mother-in-law and sister-in-law who take your order and offer pleasant conversation. When they aren't there, perhaps Dina's dad or brother will be seeing that all is well at your table. I think that the secret to the success of this tea room, which has been in operation since 1994, is it's wonderful family atmosphere...literally!

Afternoon tea, which is served on the tallest servers we have ever seen, is $13.95 CND for 1, $21.95 CND for 2 or $34.95 CND for 3. Each person enjoys salmon, cucumber and sliced egg with tomato sandwiches, buttermilk scones with Devon cream and jam, a tart, a piece of cake and tea.

For lunch you may choose a sandwich, soup, salad or one of their other specialties. Scones and tarts are sold a la carte and sticky toffee pudding is offered for $3.95 CND.

There are tea cups and saucer sets, tea pots, cozies, loose tea and other tea related items for sale in the gift area.

CM/V/Debit          Handicapped Accessible          Free Street Parking

*Hours are 11-4 Monday through Saturday. Closed Sundays and some*
*holidays. Reservations are preferred, especially for groups.*

*Proprietor's*
*Autograph_____ Date_____*

# Cottage Tea Room

*100 - 12220 Second Avenue*
*Richmond, B.C., Canada V7E 3L8*
*604-241-1853*

*From Hwy. 99, take exit 32 (Steveston Highway) west into Steveston Village.*
*Take a left at 2nd Avenue.*

We had the pleasure of spending Canada Day in Richmond and while there took time to stop in for afternoon tea at Cottage Tea Room. It is a small shop located in the heart of the village, surrounded by interesting shops and across the street from the boat docks. Though not fancy, it was very comfortable. Since it was a very busy time in town and there was so much going on, we were glad to take a break from all the activity for tea time. What we found were very friendly owners who really made an effort to make us feel welcome, as well as a tasty afternoon tea.

There are two tea sets to choose from; a cream tea for $4.25 CND and an afternoon tea which is $8.99 CND. The latter, which is served on a tiered tray, consists of finger sandwiches, scone with Devon cream & jam, a chocolate dessert and a cookie. Coffee or tea is included. If you prefer, you may choose one of the following for $5.25 CND: sausage roll or meat pie with chicken noodle soup or green pear soup or four tea sandwiches with one of the soups. Soup or a sandwich may also be order ala carte and they are priced from $2.75 to $5.50 CND, and there is a nice selection of ice cream flavors to satisfy your sweet tooth. Besides the usual English teas, Chinese and Japanese teas or available.

Cash Only          Wheelchair Accessible          Free Lot and Street Parking

*They are open 7 days a week and any time is tea time! Reservations not required. Hours are 10:30-6 except for summer when they stay open until 9.*

*Proprietor's*
*Autograph*_____*Date*_____

# The Fairmont Empress

*721 Government Street*
*Victoria, B.C., Canada V8W 1W5*
*250-389-2727*
*Emp.diningres@fairmont.com / www.fairmont.com/empress*

*Located in the Fairmont Empress Hotel in downtown Victoria, opposite the Inner Harbor and Tourist Info Center*

Whenever we meet people for the first time, and they find out that we are avid tea room visitors, the first question they always seem to ask is, "Have you been to the Empress"? We tell them that our first visit to a tearoom was at the Empress but we can't remember how long ago! Tea has been served there since 1908 so we know it wasn't in the beginning! How wonderful, though, to be able to partake of a tradition that goes back that far.

Tea is served in the sumptuous former lobby of the hotel where guests are seated at period tables and chairs or wing-backed chairs. Some tables are placed near the grand fireplace while others are set by the large picture windows that over-look the inner harbor. Regardless of where you sit, taking in the splendor of the room is an experience in itself. One last addition to the atmosphere is the pianist playing a baby grand piano during Afternoon Tea.

The Empress tea china was originally presented to King George V in 1914 and was first used by the hotel in 1939 for the Royal visit of King George VI and Queen Elizabeth. The pattern is now produced by Royal Doulton exclusively for the Empress, and is available for purchase in the Fairmont Store adjacent to the Tea Lobby. Setting off the china are silver teapots, flatware, creamers and sugar bowls and crisp white linens.

Taking tea on the Empress china makes the experience all the more special as you take time to relax and enjoy. The tea menu offerings are seasonal fruit, a selection of tea sandwiches, fruit scones with Jersey cream and strawberry preserves, elegant pastries and tea cakes. Everything is attractively arranged on tiered china and silver servers. At the end of the tea, a gift tin of Empress Blend tea is presented to each guest. The cost for this unforgettable experience is $25.95 to $49.95 CND depending on the season.

**THE Fairmont**
**EMPRESS**

MC/V/AE/DC/Checks     Wheelchair Access     Lot and Metered Parking

*Tea is daily at 12:30, 2:00 and 3:30. During the summer and on holidays there is a 5:00 seating. Reservations are recommended 5-7 days in advance during the summer and on holidays. However, walk-in's are sometimes a possibility.*

*Proprietor's*
*Autograph_____Date_____*

# The Gatsby Mansion

*309 Belleville Street*
*Victoria, B.C., Canada V8V 1X2*
*250-388-8191 / 800-563-9656 / fax 250-920-5651*
*huntingdon@bctravel.com*
*www.bctravel.com/huntingdon/gatsby.hmtl*

*Hwy. 1 (Douglas St. coming from up island)*
*Hwy 17 (Pat Bay Hwy coming from Swartz Bay Ferry*
*Terminal) Gatsby Mansion is on the same street as the*
*Parliament Building.*

This beautiful heritage mansion, with it's romantic history and lovely grounds, was the perfect place to take tea on a sunny Sunday afternoon. In good weather, you can sit on the porch and watch all the activity in the neighboring market place while enjoying a view of the Inner Harbor. Just a short walk from the harbor, we took a break in our activities to enjoy tea and conversation at a corner table inside.

The tea set was delicious and consisted of sandwiches (we had fresh salmon, chicken and cucumber), fresh fruit, scones, cakes and tarts followed by a Pernod mousse. Loved the mousse!! The tea is served in three courses and is $21.95 CND. The tea labels that they offer are Sir Thomas Lipton and Stash, though coffee is available for those who prefer. Everything was served at a leisurely pace which allowed us to enjoy our surroundings and each other.

The dining area is elegant and pleasantly appointed, with soft green walls, rather like seafoam, and pale pink tablecloths offset with white napkins and a smaller white tablecloth. The chairs inside are pink and the large windows have floor to ceiling drapery in a pink and green floral pattern! Fresh flowers, chandeliers overhead, silver and crystal give the tables the perfect finishing touch. The next time we go, we will try outside seating, as it is set up just as nicely.

While there, do take time to tour the house. There are no official tours but most of the ground floor is public space. The gardens are also worth viewing and they were the pride and joy of the original owner, William Pendray.

MC/V/AE/DC/DIS    Not Wheelchair Accessible    Street and Lot Parking

*The mansion is open year round, 24 hours a day.*
*Tea time is from 2-4 daily. Reservations are not required but are advised.*

*Proprietor's*
*Autograph_____Date_____*

# James Bay Tea Room & Restaurant

*332 Menzies Street*
*Victoria, B.C., Canada V8V 2G9*
*250-382-8282 / fax 250-389-1716*
*jamesbaytearoom@shaw.com*
*www.jamesbaytearoom.com*

*3 blocks south of the Inner Harbor and directly behind the Parliament Buildings at the corner of Menzies and Superior.*

When we found this charming neighborhood tearoom, we had no idea what awaited us once we stepped inside. As collectors of royal family memorabilia, we thought it was the closest thing to heaven! The walls are covered with pictures and paintings of the royals, and the shelves contained more of the same in book and art form. We almost forgot why we were there....but not for long! It was immediately evident that this was the place to come for afternoon tea. The room was full of customers enjoying a break from work, travelers stopping in for the tea experience and locals taking time to sit awhile with friends and neighbors. We immediately felt like the latter!

Full menu selections for breakfast and lunch are available all day, as is tea service. Breakfasts are $5.25 to $9.00 CND and lunches are $5.00 to $11.50 CDN. The choices for both are quite numerous.

There is a daily tea service which consists of finger sandwiches, scones with whipped cream and jam, tarts and your choice of tea or coffee for $10.00 CDN as well as a Sunday Brunch that includes all of the above plus home made sherry trifle for $14.00 CND. If there are children in your party, peanut butter and jam finger sandwiches are offered for either tea service as an alternate for those 12 and under.

There is a small retail shop which includes James Bay Tea Room tea shirts and postcards for sale. We were kind of eyeing some of the memorabilia on the walls!!

MC/V/AE          Wheelchair Assessable          Metered Street Parking

*Open Monday through Saturday 7-5 and Sundays 8-5. All day is "tea time". Reservations are suggested depending on day, time and number in your group. Groups of 15-30 with cancellation notice required.*

*Proprietor's*
*Autograph_____Date_____*

# *Jardin's*

5221 9th Avenue
Okanagan Falls, B.C., Canada V0H 1R0
250-497-6733 / 800-615-5553
Jardinantiques.yahoo.com / www.jardinantiques.com

*Located right on highway 97, north of Oliver and south of Penticton.*

The building where Jardin Antiques houses it's treasures is often mistaken for an original farm house. That is because Theresa and Jorry worked hard to create such a look for their very special business. The outside is painted grey with two shades of raspberry trim, and that color scheme is continued inside where the walls are a pale pink and the wood floors are well worn. Most of the display cases are old oak and glass, adding to the feel of antiquity. Collectables such as older silver tea sets and china tea pots are set among some newer gift ware, though most of the their inventory is vintage.

The garden area now boasts an extended patio where customers can take a break during their visit. This might be the perfect place to take a cup of tea, served in a real china cup, along with one of their home made scones with jam and whipped cream, or perhaps a dessert with tea would suit your fancy. Other light fare is offered including small salads, wraps, chicken kiev or stuffed chicken with broccoli and cheese.

After your break, continue browsing through the antiques, gifts and estate jewelry that Jardin's specializes in. They offer "old fashioned service with modern convenience" so enjoy your visit and take time for tea.

V/M                          Ample Lot Parking

*May 24th to September.1st, open 7 days a week. September through December, closed Fridays. Closed January 1st to May 23rd.*

*Proprietor's*
*Autograph*_____*Date*_____

# *London Heritage Farm*

*6511 Dyke Road*
*Richmond, B.C., Canada V7E 3R3*
*604-271-5220 / fax same number*
*londonhf@telus.net / City of Richmond web site*

*From Hwy 99, take exit 32 and go west on Steveston Hwy. Take left on No.2 Road then a right on Dyke Road. The farmhouse is on the right hand side of the road.*

Sometimes our tea room tours can be rather frustrating and finding this charming property was one of those times. We were in Steveston for Canada Day when someone told us about the teas at London Farm. Of course, we had to check it out! Unfortunately, they were closed that day so we were limited to walking about the beautiful grounds and peeking in the windows where tea is served. We will time it better the next time we are there!

The farm, which is owned by the City of Richmond and the London Heritage Farm Society, is a fully furnished and restored 1880's farmhouse, situated on four acres, overlooking the Fraser River. An old-fashioned tea in their heritage-style tea room offers their exclusive blend of London Lady tea, freshly baked scones with home made jam, cookies and other desserts for $5.00 CND per person. They use bone china tea cups and tea pots, lovely floral tablecloths and have "friendly service with a smile". Group teas during the week may be arranged as well as special event teas.

They ask that you visit their gift shop where they feature their tea, scone mix and home made jams as well as other items exclusive to London Farm. Call them and they will work with you in arranging tours and can give assistance to include other heritage sites in the historic Steveston Village area during your visit. The contact person is Trudean Fraser and she may be reached at the above phone number.

Cash Only          Wheelchair Accessible          Free Parking

*The house is open Wed-Sun from 10-4 during July and Aug. and Sat. and Sun. from noon to 4, Sept. through June. Reservations are recommended during the high season. Call regarding reservations and cancellation policy.*

Proprietor's
Autograph_____ Date_____

# Roedde House Museum

1415 Barclay Avenue
Vancouver, B.C., Canada V6G 1J6
604-684-7040
roeddehs@roeddehouse.org
www.roeddehouse.org

*The museum is located at the corner of Barclay and Brougham, about 2-3 blocks from Robson Street.*

Roedde House Museum was the home of Gustav and Matilda Roedde from 1893 until 1925. This beautiful heritage home has been lovingly restored and redecorated to reflect the family's life during those years. The work has been done under the direction of the Roedde House Preservation Society, which continues to maintain the home.

Though not a tea room, tea and cookies are offered in the den of this fine home, at the end of the Sunday afternoon tours. They are included in the price of admission which is $5.00 CND for adults and $4.00 CND for seniors. This is a wonderful opportunity to experience what it must have been like at the turn of the century to "take time for afternoon tea" in the parlour!

After the tour, you are invited to visit the gift shop, where you can purchase items relating to the house and it's history.

V/Checks          Wheelchair Accessible
Free Street and Lot Parking

*The Museum is open for tours Wednesday through Friday from 1-5. Tea is offered with the tour on Sundays from 2-4. Groups are welcome. Reservations are not required.*

*Proprietor's*
*Autograph*_____*Date*_____

# Secret Garden Tea Company

*5559 West Boulevard*
*Vancouver, B.C., Canada V6M 3W6*
*604-261-3075 / fax 604-261-3075*
*info@secretgardentea.com / www.secretgardentea.com*

*The nearest major cross street is 41st and West Boulevard. The tea room is*
*actually between 39th and 40th.*

Judging from the number of people having tea or lunch the day we visited, this tea room isn't really a secret! There were those who seemed to be enjoying a break from work, others treating their grandchildren to tea , friends taking time for a visit, and others, like ourselves, just enjoying that respite called afternoon tea. We chose a quiet table in the corner but there were overstuffed chairs and couches in front of the fireplace, as well. Flowers and plants decorated the room as did tea related gift items, which fit in nicely. Shelves near the middle of the room housed the extensive selection of Secret Garden loose leaf teas.

Gourmet sandwiches, which are served with crisp organic greens, are $8.95 and $9.95, and there are a number of salad choices for $6.95 and $9.95. Specialty item such as chicken pot pie, torte and garden omelette are also $9.95. For the lighter appetite, there are two soup choices priced at $4.25.

The tea menu offers three choices, from the Mini High Tea, which consists of three miniature sweets, one miniature scone, raspberry jam, Devon cream and Secret Garden Tea for $8.95 to the Demi Tea, a sampling of the High tea for $10.95 and the High Tea itself for $19.95. High Tea is served on an elegant tiered server and includes miniature pastries, sweets, sweet scones, Devon cream, raspberry jam, tea sandwiches and a piping hot pot of tea. We enjoyed a leisurely afternoon with delicious food and a very nice visit with the owners.

All prices Canadian.

MC/V/Debit          Wheelchair Access          Metered Street Parking

*Open Monday to Saturday 8-7 and Sundays 9-6. Reservations required for*
*High Tea service which is served at 12:00, 2:00 and 4:00 every day. There is*
*a maximum of 20 people for group reservation. Parties of 8 or more must*
*reserve with a credit card and a 15% gratuity is added.*

*Proprietor's*
*Autograph_____Date_____*

# Silk Road Aromatherapy and Tea Co.

1624 Government Street
Victoria, B.C., Canada V8W 1Z3
250-704-2688
silkroad@silkroad.tea / www.silkroadtea.com

*If you are driving south on Blanshard St. or Douglas St., turn right on Fisgard, then left on Government St. It is near the Gates to Chinatown on the corner of Fisgard and Government.*

Sometimes you just want a good cup of tea and this is just the place to fill that desire. Though primarily a mail order business, customers are welcome to stop for a pot of tea in their "tea oasis", a small seating area in the front window of their retail store.

They describe themselves as importers and blenders of premium quality loose teas, which they retail and wholesale. Throughout the year they conduct tea tastings, traditional Japanese tea ceremonies and other tea related events. You can check their website to find out dates and times.

If tea is what you want, tea is just what you get at Silk Road.

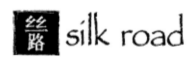

*Monday through Saturday 10-6 and Sunday 12 - 5.*

Proprietor's
Autograph_____Date_____

# *Sweet Revenge Patisserie*

4160 Main Street
Vancouver, B.C., Canada V5V 3P7
604-879-7933
sweet-revenge@shaw.ca / www.sweet-revenge.ca

*From Hwy 99, turn east onto East King Edward Ave.
Turn right on main. They are at E. 26th Avenue.*

This is the kind of place you seek out when really craving something wonderful and sweet to have with your tea. The Edwardian décor makes you feel special as you gaze upon lush red wallpapers, oil lamps, antique style furniture, soft wood floors and faux tin ceiling. The surroundings, as well as the background music by such artists as Billie Holiday or Benny Goodman, invite you to make yourself at home and stay awhile.

Everything is made fresh daily in their bakery by one of the owners, Grant, and is guaranteed to be up to your expectations. Some of the choices are so decadent and interesting that you enjoy them in a leisurely manner, much like a pot of your favorite tea. Just a teaser...you can find zuccotto, crème brulee, white chocolate cheese cake and pear bread pudding among your choices. Any of those goes well with a cup of tea! Prices range from $4.95 to $6.95 CND.

Speaking of tea, there are over 2 dozen fine loose leaf teas to choose from, including the house tea "Belgian Chocolate Revenge Rooibos". Bulk tea is also available under the Metropolitan label.

Because the hours are so accommodating, you may choose to stop in for a mid-morning snack or perhaps a little something to follow your evening meal. Which ever you choose, you will not be disappointed.

Cash Only    Wheelchair Accessible    Metered and Lot Parking

*Sunday, Monday and Thursday open 7pm to 12 am. Friday and Saturday open 7 pm to 1 am. Closed Tuesday and Wednesday.*

*Proprietor's
Autograph*_____*Date*_____

# The White Heather Tea Room

*1885 Oak Bay Avenue*
*Victoria, B.C., Canada V8R 1C6*

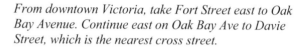

*From downtown Victoria, take Fort Street east to Oak*
*Bay Avenue. Continue east on Oak Bay Ave to Davie*
*Street, which is the nearest cross street.*

Soft pastel walls, fresh flowers and beautiful white linen table clothes set the tone for this special Scottish themed tea room. Though there isn't a tartan to be seen, Agnes has given her room a unique feel with large Tea Clipper Ship prints as well as botanical art work by Charles Dool. White china and glassware as well as floral draperies on the expansive windows complete the bright and cheery décor.

There are three tea selections to chose from. The Wee Tea at $9.25 CND per person consists of 2 tea sandwiches, mini cheese scone with chicken apple filling, slice of tea loaf, and a piece of delicious Scottish Shortbread. The Not So Wee Tea offers a selection of tea sandwiches, freshly bakes scone with Delicious preserves and Devon cream, mini cheese scone with chicken apple filling, savoury tart of the day and a lovely selection of fresh baking for $13.75 CND per person. The Big Muckle Giant Tea For Two includes a selection of tea sandwiches, freshly baked scones with delicious preserves and Devon cream, mini smoked salmon and cream cheese scone-wich with pepper jelly, savoury tart of the day, cheese krispie with cream cheese and apple jelly, savoury surprise of the day, and a wonderful selection of fresh baking for $33.95 CND for two people. Just typing this reminds me why we don't have breakfast or dinner on tea day!!

Besides the tea menu, light breakfast items are offered from 9:30 - 11 and luncheon items such as soup, salads and sandwiches are available as well. Fresh baking changes daily, as they are constantly making new creations…."to make you more cuddly".

Tea cozies as well as 22 different loose leaf teas may be purchased. Themed teas such as Christmas and Valentines Day are presented.

MC/V/DC          Wheelchair Accessible          1 hr. Street Parking and Lot

Hours of operation are Tuesday through Saturday 9:30 to 5. Tea is served from 1:30 to 5. Reservations are required with a one day advance notice. Available to groups from 15 to 30 people.

*Proprietor's*
*Autograph*_____*Date*_____

# *Windsor House Tea Room*
## *and Restaurant*
*2340 Windsor Road*
*Victoria, B.C., Canada V8S 3E9*
*250-595-3135*

*Take Hwy. 17 South. Turn left on Johnson-Oak/Bay Avenue. Continue onto Newport then turn left on Windsor Road. The Oak Bay Marina is one block west.*

The tea room and restaurant are located in an old Tudor Style townhouse which has been converted into a charming and tranquil setting for afternoon tea. Private rooms are set up in a manner that allows you to feel that the space is all your own. Cute and quaint décor abounds with floral wallpaper, cottage windows and beautiful aging wood add to the soothing feeling that envelops you as you sit and enjoy a cup of piping hot tea with friends.

Traditional High Tea is offered all day for $29.95 CND for two and includes such items as tea sandwiches, scones, Devon cream, jam, fruit and dainty tea desserts. For those whose tastes go toward a different type of fare, delicious English style meals are also offered. Groups are welcome and outside catering is available.

Tea pots and tea cozies are available for purchase.

MV/V/AE/Debit          Wheelchair Accessible          Street and Lot Parking

*Open Monday through Saturday 8-4*
*Reservations are recommended with 24 hour notice. Groups are welcome.*

*Proprietor's*
*Autograph*_____*Date*_____

129

# *Welcome*
# *to*
# *Beyond*
# *the*
# *Northwest*

# The Arizona Biltmore
## Resort & Spa

2400 East Missouri Avenue
Phoenix, Arizona 98016
602-955-6600 / 800-950-0086
reservations@arizonabiltmore.com
www.arizonabiltmore.com

This was the first tea room we visited on our Spring Break tour of Phoenix tea rooms, and we headed straight here from the airport. Unfortunately, tea time was later in the afternoon so we had to make reservations and return at the appointed time. No problem, we just went to another tea room for awhile!

The Biltmore, a Frank Lloyd Wright creation, is such a fabulous place that it is impossible to describe it. Just think of the movies of the 40's which featured fabulous resorts and you have the picture. Opening in 1929 this hotel actually was a haven for the rich and famous including Clark Gable and every president since Herbert Hoover. On the weekend we were there, I was thrilled to find out that the NFL owners and coaches were having a meeting there! Believe it or not, two of my loves are tea and the San Francisco 49ers.

Trivia aside, this was one of the best teas that we have ever had. It was served in the lobby of the hotel on low tables set by cushy sofa's and chairs, or at intimate tea tables. Linens and silver were set on the table and pretty floral china with matching tea pot and silver tiered servers finished off the formal appearance. Our tea, which was priced at $32.50 per person, was presented in three courses. The buttermilk scones, Devon cream, jam and Dundee cake were served first. That was followed by mesquite smoked salmon, Black Forest ham, turkey and roast vegetable with goat cheese and olive sandwiches, crab salad puffs, and curried chicken salad. The dessert selection was raspberry filled tart, mocha swan puff, lemon tart, crème brulee, chocolate pot du cream, frangipani tea cake, lintzer torte cookie and chocolate strawberry. Thank you chef Holster and hostess Sylvia for visiting with us!

Please know that a tea like this is our only meal for the day! It was John's mom Charlotte's first tea room experience and it was a wonderful choice.

*Tea is served every afternoon at 2:30 in the lobby.*

*Proprietor's*
*Autograph*_____ *Date*_____

# Gooseberries

*13216 N. 7th Street*
*Phoenix, Arizona 85022*
*602-789-0622*
*store@gooseberries.net / www.gooseberries.net*

Located in a strip mall, Gooseberries is very easy to find...just look for the crisp green awning and bold green letters. Parking is unlimited and this is a plus when you spend up to two hours enjoying afternoon tea! The name intrigued us so of course, we asked about the origin. The owner, Kathleen, shared that she, "stole gooseberries from a neighbors yard when she was a child living in Pennsylvania", hence, the name!

We visited here late in the afternoon after another tea room visit (we visit two a day when on a tour!), so chose lighter fare and shared it. We do this so we can have the tea room experience without eating ourselves into oblivion!

Kathleen offered a luncheon tea for $15.00 which included three open-faced sandwiches made with tomato and watercress, crunchy chicken salad and tuna with dill and veggies. The scones were served in a basket and there were two flavors - plain and cinnamon/nut. Devon cream and lemon curd accompanied the scones. The dessert was tiramisu, which I love and we all thoroughly enjoyed.

The tea area is set along one side of the building and the rest of the area is a wonderful gift and specialty shop. The décor is a little bit Southwest with peach colored walls and aqua accents. There is a strong garden theme and a large amount of the gifts are garden related. Of course, other items are available including enough tea accoutrements to tempt me. Perhaps you will choose to do as we did and browse while enjoying your tea then shop before leaving the store!

*Afternoon tea is served Tuesday through Saturday at 3:00 by reservation.*

*Proprietor's*
*Autograph*_____*Date*_____

133

# Serendipity Tea Room

3601 E. Indian School Road
Phoenix, Arizona 85918
602-957-4203 / fax 602-957-5448
www.serendipitytearoom.com

*Located at the S.E. corner of Indian School and 36th Street.*

This was near our "old stomping grounds ", as we lived off Indian School back in the early '70's when we were stationed at Luke AFB. Being so close to our former home gave us an opportunity to check it out and reminisce a bit after our tea room visit.

Serendipity was a very special place to take tea. Situated in the back corner of a huge antiques mall, the "room" was completely transformed into a very inviting and peaceful oasis. Half walls were constructed with "windows" atop them. The windows were adorned with Battenberg lace curtains and vases of flowers sat on the sills. Floral cloths with lace toppers covered the tables and the dishes and servers were all vintage china. There was a beautifully appointed separate room available for parties or groups. The owner, Joann, a former health care worker, had a dream and it became a reality when she opened Serendipity in 2001. She can be proud of her accomplishment, as her tea room was voted Best Tea Room in Phoenix that same year.

The Afternoon Tea menu is set and the cost is $16.95 plus gratuity. We had a wonder selection which was served in three courses, the first being cranberry scones with Chantilly cream and lemon curd. Next we were treated to tomato basil, cucumber, bacon/parsley and tuna spinach sandwiches, a chicken curry tart, a bunny shaped apricot/pecan sandwich and a mini quiche. The final course, a selection of desserts, was presented on a beautiful green pedestal server. Those indulgences were a mint cream filled chocolate cup, an apricot bar, chocolate gingerbread cookie, cream puff, poppy seed shortbread cookie and a strawberry fan. Lest you think we over-indulged, three of us shared a tea for two!!

Enjoy your tea but allow plenty of time to browse the antiques area.

*Restaurant hours are Tues. through Sat. 11-5. Tea is offered from 1:30 - 4 and reservations are required 24 hours in advance. Lunch as well as Afternoon Tea is offered.*

*Proprietor's*
*Autograph_____Date_____*

# The Spicey

*7141 N. 59th Avenue*
*Glendale, Arizona 85301*
*623-937-6534*
*webmaster@historic-glendale.net*
*www.historic-glendale.net/spicery.htm*

*Located in the historic area of Glendale*

The second day of our jaunt through Phoenix brought us to this very interesting historic old area of Glendale. The streets are lined with antique and collectable stores, quaint specialty shops, interesting older building, and intimate dining places. Of course, we chose a tea room for our lunch experience!

The Spicery is located on the edge of the historic district in a cottage style home, painted in shades of yellow on the outside with paned windows covered with floor to ceiling lace on the inside. Thought the space is small, there are four rooms which serve as dining rooms and the original kitchen has been converted to an efficient work space. The walls are covered with a pretty floral pattern and the draperies, which set off the lace, are in coordination prints. The assorted tables are covered in lace and fresh flowers were poised on every table.

The tea set was presented in courses with the first course consisting of small samples of blueberry bread, pound cake, shortbread, cinnamon roll and a scone with cinnamon flavored cream. The main course was served on a tiered server and offered cucumber sandwich, ham biscuit, chicken sandwich, quiche and a tuna round. For the finale we enjoyed a slice of nut bread, a cream puff and my favorite...strawberry trifle! The cost was $12.00 and the tip and tax were added on.

Besides Afternoon Tea, lunch is offered and the salads and sandwiches looked very good. The majority of their customers seemed to be lunch diners though we met some other "tea people" with whom we had a lively conversation. Tea people really are the friendliest people!

*Reservations required 48 hours in advance.*

*Proprietor's*
*Autograph*_____*Date*_____

135

# The Teeter House

622 E. Adams Street
Phoenix, Arizona 85004
602-252-4682 / Fax 602-534-1786
www.theteeterhouse.com

*This tea room is located in Historic Heritage Square. Take 7th St. to Van Buren then take a right to parking on 5th Street.*

This was the last day of our tour and we ended it on a very high note. Built in 1911, Elizabeth Teeter purchased the boarding house in 1919 and lived in it until 1965. The new owner, Lynn, purchased the tea room in 1999 after attending the Scottsdale Culinary Institute. Her very capable server the day we were there was Nick, a charming and fun young man from *Eugene, Oregon*!

Since becoming a tea room, the house now plays hostess to guests in each of the first floor tea rooms which are decorated in period wall papers, lace and drapery covered windows, and interesting wall décor. There is also a comfortable enclosed porch in the back which is used in the summer. Most of the decorations are for sale and there is a small gift shop in the lobby area.

Our tea, which was the Afternoon Tea, was generous and delicious. For $14.95, we enjoyed a basket of heart-shaped raisin scones with Devon cream, four types of "un-ending" sandwiches, three types of fruit, sugared nuts, petite fours and bottomless pots of tea. There were other teas available from the cream tea for $6.95 to the traditional English High Tea, which varies in price depending on the menu. It is served in the evening and includes meat dishes, potatoes, soup, salad, a pint of ale and dessert. Other teas are the Garden Tea consisting of assorted tea sandwiches, seasonal fruit, and shortbread with lemon curd or scones with Devon cream for $10.95 and the Children's Tea which has assorted finger sandwiches, fruit, lemonade and a cookie with cream for $5.95.

To say we had a good time is an understatement. The owner was charming, the server a delight and our surroundings pleasant and relaxing. Heritage Square was fun to explore after our tea and it was well worth the time spent looking for Teeter House.

*Open Tues. through Sat. 11-4 and Sun. 12-4. Reservations for afternoon tea are accepted. Lunch is served until 3:30. High Tea is served on the third Thursday of the month 5:30-8:30. Reservations required. Use the parking garage and ask to have your parking receipt validated.*

*Proprietor's*
*Autograph*_____*Date*_____

# Tessa's Tea and Treasures

4700 N. Central Avenue
Phoenix, Arizona 85012
602-234-3422
tessatea@cs.com / www.tessatea.com

This was the second tea room we went to on our tea room tour in Phoenix. Because we were having tea later at the Biltmore, we elected to just have a scones and a pot of tea. The scone was scrumptious and was presented in a most attractive manner with a side of chocolate dipped strawberries.

We had an opportunity to spend some time with the owner, Patti, and learned that the tea room is named for her daughter, Tessa. She has been in business for 10 years and shares space with a wonderful antiques and collectables mall. Some tea tables are set out in the antiques area so you can eye some treasures while you sip. The tea room is located in a single level cream colored stucco building with brown trim, which is surrounded by a wrought iron fence, palm trees and other greenery. It is on a very busy street but was very easy to find.

Though we didn't have tea, we were able to view the tea sets at other tables and they looked marvelous! Tessa's offers a Tea Plate, which is a light sampling of Afternoon Tea, for $8.95 and includes a scone, tea sandwiches and desserts but not tea. There are two other sets, the first being the Afternoon Tea. It offers tea and fresh baked scones with Devonshire cream, lemon curd & jam, tea sandwiches and miniature desserts for $14.95. A three course High Tea includes choice of soup or salad with fresh baked dinner scones, tea sandwiches, mini quiches, mini meat pies, sandwiches and a dessert tray including the special dessert of the day and tea for $17.95. Special teas may be requested for birthdays, showers meetings and special occasions.

You are invited to dress-up in one of the many hats, pairs of gloves or a piece of vintage jewelry should the mood strike! After your tea break, allow yourself time to walk the many aisles of the antique store before heading out to reality.

Wheel Chair Accessible                    Lot Parking

*Reservations are required for tea. This is a restaurant as well as a tea room.*

Proprietor's
Autograph_____Date_____

# Westgate Plaza Hotel

*1055 Second Avenue*
*San Diego, California 92117*
*619-238-1818*

Spring Break, again, and we headed out of town to visit tea rooms in southern California, where the weather was beautiful and the vacation relaxing. San Diego has so much to offer that visiting tea rooms was just one of the many adventures we sought out. We were only there for three days so opted to have tea only once a day...not counting a morning cuppa at the Japanese Tea Garden at Balboa Park!

The Westgate Plaza was our first tea stop and a true pleasure at that. The hotel, built in 1970, is in the center of downtown and it is an elegant work of art, both inside and out. Tea is served daily in the magnificent lobby, where you sit on luxurious couches and chairs covered in ivory hued brocade or at beautifully appointed tables. The center of the tea area showcases an oversized arrangement of pink and cream colored flowers and each table is graced with a vase of fresh red roses. Crystal chandeliers and gilt finished mirrors and wall adornments add to the opulence as do the antique furnishings. A harpist or pianist, playing softly in the background, adds to the ambiance. Can one ask for better surroundings for afternoon tea?

The place setting includes beautiful silver flatware and china dishes, as well as blue glass water goblets. Everything is served individually to you from silver trays by the tea host. The first course included watercress, roast beef and chestnut sandwiches, and turkey & salmon rolls. Then scones were served with lemon curd and cream. This was followed by mini desserts of meringue tart, chocolate dipped strawberry, mocha mousse square, raspberry mousse cake and lemon mousse square. The final course was a silver goblet of sliced strawberries topped with chantilly cream. We were treated like royalty and this wonderful afternoon of indulgence was offered at $14.00 per person. I recommend that when you visit the city, find time to visit the Plaza.

*Served daily from 2:30 to 5:00. Reservations are required. Use the parking garage and ask to have your parking receipt validated.*

*Proprietor's*
*Autograph*_____*Date*_____

# Mrs. Burton's

2465 Heritage Park Row
San Diego, California 92110
619-294-4600
chappete@aol.com
www.mrsburtonstearoom.com

*Located next to Old Towne San Diego.*

This charming tea room is located at Heritage Park, amid similar period houses which were moved there to recreate a turn of the century neighborhood. This particular home is a Classic Revival, with pediments and dentil cornices. As you walk the street, you really get a feel for what it would have been like to chat with a neighbor over the fence, pay a visit to the doctor, stop by the milliner's shop or take time for afternoon tea at Mrs. Burton's.

The tea room offers a wonderful tea set during which each cup of tea is served to you...no tea pot on the table. The tiered servers were adorned with silk flowers and beautiful ribbons, and the napkin rings were individual flower holders. As for the food, it was served quickly and everything was attractive and delicious. Our set consisted of cranberry scones which were served with carrot/nut, cucumber, pineapple cream, salmon, sun-dried tomato and chicken salad sandwiches. Grapes, a lemon bar, peanut butter cake, strawberries, orange cake and a chocolate brownie completed the tea, all for $18.95 per person.

Besides the tea room, Mrs. Burtons houses Country Craftsman of San Diego which offers hand crafted items, wedding accessories, Victorian style dresses, hats, candles, Christmas ornaments and both baby and Shaker furniture. If you have forgotten your hat, there is a selection of men's and women's available for you to borrow. John was very dapper in his top hat and I complimented it with the biggest red hat I could find!

If you visit Old Towne, as most visitors do, be sure to allow yourself time for afternoon tea and browsing the gift shop. Henry and Judy will extend a very warm welcome! A visit to Mrs. Burton's in Heritage Park and Old Towne San Diego is a day long adventure not to be missed!

*Judy offers a choice of party themes and favors including - Baby Shower, Beanie Baby, Birthday, Bridal and Children's. Walk-in's are welcome but reservations are recommended.*

*Proprietor's*
*Autograph*_____*Date*_____

139

# U.S. Grant Hotel

## A Wyndham Historic Hotel

326 Broadway
San Diego, California 92101
619-744-2062 / fax 619-232-3626

*Located in downtown San Diego on Broadway between 3rd and 4th.*

It was the last day of our visit to San Diego so we really had to rush to get in one more tea room visit. We chose the U.S. Grant Hotel, which is in the heart of downtown. Tea is served in the massive lobby of this hotel, which was built by Ulysses S. Grant, Jr., son of the former president. The hotel has undergone a great deal of renovation but we are so glad that this priceless piece of antiquity is still standing. Unfortunately, the home of the former president was demolished!

We arrived at the end of tea time but the hostess graciously offered to "put something together" for us. We were seated at a small, cloth covered table, and were immediately brought a pot of tea. While seated, we were able to take in the beautiful surroundings of dark green carpets on well manicured wood floors, burgundy and green walls, and lush greenery, especially potted palms. A grand piano was is place to entertain tea sippers but, alas, we were too late to enjoy the music.

The dishes, serving pieces, tea cups and teapots were the lovely and recognizable Royal Albert "Old English Rose". Each course was served separately on fresh china and everything was tasty and nicely presented. The first course brought four sandwich selections - salmon, cucumber, turkey and egg salad. This was followed by a small scone and a crumpet served with Devon cream and a selection of jams. The final dessert course consisted of a chocolate covered strawberry, blackberry cream tart, mandarin cream tart and mocha cannoli. The bottomless tea was served with heart shaped sugar cubes, a memorable touch. All this, along with exceptional service, was $16.95 per person.

*Like most hotels, tea is served in the afternoon, usually between 2 and 5. Please call the hotel for hours and days.*

Proprietor's
Autograph_____ Date_____

140

# Welcome

## to

## Tea

## at Sea

# Norwegian Sky
*Norwegian Cruise Lines*

It is very special to be able to partake of High Tea while at sea. Norwegian Cruise Lines offers one High Tea on their eight day cruise from Seattle, Washington up into the Inside Passage and it is quite nice. Le Bistro, one of the nicer restaurants, was the location of our tea, which was served at 4:00 pm sharp.

Our daughter and son-in-law accompanied us on this cruise, so Alicia had the opportunity to enjoy "tea at sea' with us. Each cruise line has it's own way of presenting tea and Norwegian offered one that was served. The central table, which was covered with red linens, was laden with numerous silver trays which held the tea offerings and the silver tea pots. The servers passed the trays, one at a time, and we selected whatever item we wished to try. The tea menu consisted of turkey or roast beef triple decked sandwiches, raisin scones with whipped cream and strawberry jam, palmiers, raspberry tarts and strawberry tortes. Everything was delicious and the service was just great.

The tables were covered in white linens and the napkins matched perfectly. Fresh flowers served as centerpieces. Our plates were white with a burnt red border, and the cups and saucers were a rather heavy pottery type in a reddish color. The tea was Sir Thomas Lipton Darjeeling (a favorite tea of mine!), and it was served continuously during the tea.

The experience was definitely good and something I look forward each time we cruise.

# MS Westerdam
*Holland America Lines*

Holland America offers tea at 3:30 every day on their cruises. Afternoon tea on the Westerdam was served in the dining room and you were welcome to sit where ever you pleased...no assigned seating for tea!

The tables were set with white linens and small vases of fresh flowers. The fine china plates, cups and saucers were used. Servers passed silver trays of treats starting with sandwiches made of turkey, egg salad and chicken salad. They were followed by small scones with jam and cream. The last course, which was petite desserts, consisted of cookies, tarts and small cakes. Tea was offered frequently and the other menu items were passed a number of times.

Everything was delicious and the service was superb; just as we would expect on a Holland America cruise.

# MS Maasdam

*Holland America Lines*
*Afternoon Tea*

On a recent cruise with a number of other Red Hat Society members, we had the opportunity to take Afternoon Tea every day from 3:30 to 4:00 in the Explorers Lounge. It was especially nice to take tea on this cruise, as you never knew which other Red Hatters would show up! The Explorers Lounge is one of the more formal lounges on the ship, and there is a grand piano on a platform where a trio entertained us each day as we chatted over tea. It is also a open lounge from which we could take in the beauty of Alaska through the massive windows that banked the room.

Low tables were set with white linens and individual place settings of white china. You selected your tea from a Lipton tea chest, then small individual pots were brought to the table. Servers passed silver trays of sandwiches and they were all open faced mini bagels. The selections were cucumber with olive, roast beef, salmon or turkey. There were no scones at Afternoon Tea but the dessert assortment was extensive. No, I didn't try them all but I did check them all out! I had the strawberry mousse, swan puff and chocolate chip cookie and they were delicious.

Though I did not make it to tea every day, I thoroughly enjoyed the days that I did. Thanks Nancy, Claudia, Suzy and Dorothy for the company!

# MS Maasdam

*Holland America Lines*
*High Tea*

One very special High Tea is offered during an eight day Holland America Cruise and I made sure I did not miss it. To say that it was spectacular is an under-statement! It was a work of art...almost too pretty to destroy.

As we entered the dining room, a sea of huge silver trays and beautiful flowers greeted us. Linen covered tables were covered with every imaginable tea offering we could think of and servers were there to help us make our selections.

When there was so much to choose from, it was difficult to choose just what items I wanted to try so I just tried some things that seemed special or a little different. For savories I had the chicken a la king which was served in mini pastry shells and the shrimp on crostini. I did not have any sandwiches but did choose the turkey on a mini roll and of course, a cream scone. My dessert selections were a linzer cookie, mini cheese cake and a petite fruit tart. John selected some different items, which I will share with you. He had a sausage roll, cucumbers on a mini roll, cream scones, chocolate dipped strawberry, petite strawberry tart, petite custard éclair, macaroon, mini mocha torte and pecan pie bar. Believe it or not, these are a small sampling of what was available on the buffet! Such good food that looked so beautiful!

During the cruise I had the opportunity to interview the Executive Chef, Markus Jenni, and that was a wonderful experience. He was charming and so forthcoming with answers to my questions about his background and the cruise ship experience. He is from Switzerland, which may explain why the chocolate confections were so wonderful. His experiences prior to running a cruise ship kitchen included working in the kitchens of fine hotels and supervising the kitchen at a golf and country club. In the dessert section you will find some great recipes which he shared with me. Enjoy, and remember, when cruising, never miss the opportunity to take tea.

*Welcome*

*to*

*Favorite*

*Recipes*

# Beverages

# Ginger Lemonade
## Betty Crocker website
© 2003 General Mills, Inc.

3 cups sugar
16 cups (4 quarts) water
12 to 14 slices gingerroot (about 2 inch piece)
4 cups fresh lemon juice (24 lemons)
2 lemons sliced

Mix sugar water and gingerroot in 8 qt. Dutch oven. Heat to boiling, stirring occasionally. Remove from heat and cool 15 minutes. Remove gingerroot.

Pour sugar mixture into pitcher or large glass or plastic container. Stir in lemon juice and refrigerate at least one hour until chilled.

Serve lemonade over ice with lemon slices.

# Lemonade Tea

## Betty Crocker website
© 2003 General Mills, Inc.

2 cans (12oz. each) thawed frozen lemonade concentrate
3 quarts iced tea
Fresh mint sprigs, if desired

Make lemonade according to directions on can, using a punch bowl or other large container. Stir in tea.

Serve over ice. Garnish with mint

# Zesty

# Butterscotch Tea

### Queen Jill

1 cup of hot tea
2 butterscotch hard candies
1 tbsp. honey
1/2 tsp. lemon juice
1 cinnamon stick

To the cup of tea add butterscotch, honey, lemon juice and cinnamon. Stir until the candies melt, or remove the remaining pieces before drinking.

"Ooh so good!!"

# Tea Recipes
## "Silk Road"
## Victoria, BC. Canada

## Black Tea / The' Noir
### Ceylon Black Tea/Bergamot Fruit Essence

Canton orange recipe ideas:

Classic iced tea: brew 1 Tbsp. tea in 2 cups boiling water. Steep 5 min. and strain over ice or chill for 4 hours.

Shangri-la: mix chilled tea with equal parts of peach juice. Garnish with fresh peach or orange slices.

Dream Palace: mix hot tea with white or dark hot chocolate. Top with whopped cream and chocolate shavings.

## Herbal Tea / Tisane
### Peppermint Tea

West Coast peppermint recipe ideas:

Classic iced tea: brew 1 tbsp. tea in 2 cups boiling water. Steep for 10 minutes and strain over ice or chill for 4 hours.

West Coast Breeze: follow above method. Mix chilled tea with equal parts lemonade or grapefruit juice.

West Coast trail: brews 1 tsp. tea in 1/2 cup water. Steep 5 minutes and strain into 1/2 cup hot white or dark chocolate. Serve with whipped cream.

Frosty's Snow Melt: pour hot tea over vanilla or mint ice cream. Serve immediately.

# Sandwiches, Savories and Soups

# Favorite Sandwiches
### "Anna's Tea Room"
### Coupeville, Washington

## Asparagus Rolls

Cut crusts off white bread; flatten bread with open palm of hand or roll lightly with rolling pin. Spread with mayonnaise and lay spear of well-drained canned asparagus spear on bread, with stem end even with one end of bread. If spear overhangs bread, bend tip end back over rest of spear. Roll. Let rest overnight or several hours in fridge, covered with wrung out dampened paper towel, then saran wrap.

## Pickled Beets and Cheddar

Spread whole wheat bread lightly with butter. Cover with *thinly* sliced Cheddar cheese and cover with well drained pickled beet slices. Top with another layer of *thinly* sliced Cheddar and another slice of lightly buttered bred. Trim crusts and cut into squares. Best made just before serving with VERY well drained beets.

## Aloha Spread

This spread is great for using up crushed pineapple left over from other recipes. Combine 6 oz. cream cheese, 2 oz. finely shredder Cheddar cheese and 2 or 3 oz. very well-drained crushed pineapple. Spread on whole wheat bread, trim crusts and cut into triangles or ribbons. This also goes well with thinly sliced ham. If using ham, it's easier to cut into squares.

# Bell Pepper Cheddar Chowder

### "Anna's Tea Room"
### Coupeville, Washington

1/2 cup butter or margarine
1 red bell pepper, chopped (plus some for garnish)
1 yellow bell pepper, chopped (plus some for garnish)
1/2 cup chopped carrot
1/2 cup sliced celery
1/2 cup chopped onion
2 cloves garlic, minced
1/2 cup all purpose flour
1 quart half and half
5 tsp. vegetable base
2 1/2 cups water
1 (12oz) can beer
1/2 tsp. dried mustard
1/4 tsp. dried rosemary, crushed
1/4 tsp. salt
1/4 tsp. ground red pepper
1/4 tsp. freshly ground black pepper
2 cups (8oz.) shredded sharp Cheddar cheese
Garnishes: fresh rosemary, finely chopped peppers

Melt butter in a large Dutch oven over medium-high heat. Add chopped peppers, carrots, celery, onion and garlic. Cook, stirring constantly, 5 minutes or until tender. Add flour, stirring constantly. Cook 1 minute, stirring constantly. Gradually add half and half, vegetable base, water and beer. Cook, stirring constantly until thickened and bubbly. Stir in mustard, rosemary, salt and peppers. Gradually add cheese, stirring until cheese melts. Garnish as desired and serve immediately.

### Yield: 11 cups

# Cheese & Carrot Tea Sandwiches

*"A Year of Teas at the Elmwood Inn"*
*by Shelley and Bruce Richardson*

1 cup grated carrots
1 cup grated sharp cheddar cheese
5 tbsp. mayonnaise
slices whole wheat bread
salt and pepper to taste
thin sliced carrots
fresh parsley

Mix together carrots, cheese, mayonnaise, salt and pepper. Remove crusts from bread and cut out round pieces with a small cutter. Spread slices of brad with cheese mixture. Garnish with a thin slice of carrot and fresh parsley.

Makes 32 open faced sandwiches

# Chicken Salad
### "Vintage Inn B & B"
### Vancouver, Washington

2 boneless, skinless chicken breasts, frozen
2 sprigs fresh rosemary
1/2 tsp. Johnny's seasoning salt
1 stalk celery, finely chopped
1/2 cup dried cranberries, chopped
1/4 cup finely chopped almonds
11 oz. can mandarin orange segments, chopped
1/2 cup mayonnaise

Place frozen chicken breasts in an electric skillet set at 250'. Sprinkle with seasoning salt and place 1 sprig of rosemary on top of each breast. Cover with lid and cook for 8 minutes. Turn meat over and cook for another 8 minutes or until done and no longer pink inside. You may add 1/4 cup water after turning the meat to prevent sticking. After the meat is done, remove it from the pan, set aside and cool completely. After the meat is cooled, dice meat thoroughly and put in a medium mixing bowl. Mix in the remaining ingredients. Cover and let chill for a couple of hours or overnight to allow the flavors to blend.

Use as a salad or sandwich filling

# Chicken Salad
# Florentine Sandwich
### "The Teazone"
### Portland, Oregon

### Chicken Salad Florentine

16 oz. cubed cooked white chicken meat
2 - 10 oz. pkgs. frozen chopped spinach, thawed and
thoroughly squeezed dry
1 package Knoor's vegetable soup mix
1 cup light mayonnaise
1/2 can drained and chopped water chestnuts

Blend all the ingredients and let it sit for two hours before serving. If available, serve on an Artisan style crusty white bread. Serve with a side salad and you're all set!

# Crispies
## "Oregon Tea Garden"
### Silverton, Oregon

Flour tortilla
1 lime (lemon may be used)
Garlic salt (celery or onion work)
Olive oil
Sprinkle of cheese (optional)

Zest and juice the lime. Wisk the lime juice and zest with about 4 tbsp. olive oil. Add about a tsp of garlic salt or more if you like your food saltier. Cut about 3 large tortillas or several small ones into fun shapes with a cookie cutter or into pie wedges with a scissors. Dip the tortillas into the mixture. Shake off excess oil. Place on cookie sheet in 350' oven until golden. Place on paper towels to absorb any excess oil and serve with soup or salad.

*Michele says, "create and enjoy!"*

# Cucumber and Roquefort Cheese Sandwiches

*"Afternoon Tea Serenade"*
*Recipes from Famous Tea Rooms*
*Classical Chamber Music*
*by Sharon O'Connor*

10 thin whole wheat bread slices
2 cucumbers, peeled and cut into thin slices

Roquefort Cheese Mousse

8 oz. Roquefort cheese
8 oz. Cream cheese at room temperature
4 tbsp. butter at room temperature
1/4 cup walnuts, roasted
1/2 tsp. black sesame seeds

Preheat the oven to 350'. Place the bread slices on a baking sheet and toast them in the preheated oven for 5 minutes. Trim the cucumber to the same length as the bread.

To make the mousse: In a blender or food processor, blend the Roquefort cheese, cream cheese, and butter until smooth. Spread a layer of the mixture evenly over each piece of toast. Place overlapping slices of cucumber on the toast. Trim off the bread crusts and cut the bread into triangles. Garnish each sandwich with a piped rosette of Roquefort cheese mousse and some toasted walnuts. To finish, sprinkle with black sesame seeds.

Makes 20 tea sandwiches

# Deviled Ham and Gherkins
## "All the Tea in China"
### by Yvonne Wrightman

6.5 oz. can deviled ham
1 cup cottage cheese
2 tbsp. minced gherkins
salt and pepper
12 slices rye or pumpernickel bread

Combine ham, cheese, gherkins, salt and pepper, and mix well. Spread half the bread slices with the mixture. Top with remaining slices. Wrap in plastic wrap and refrigerate. Slice off crusts and serve.

# Miniature Quiches

"Breakfast at Nine, Tea at Four"
Favorite Recipes from
Cape May's Mainstay Inn
by Sue Carroll

Pastry

1 cup softened butter
8 oz. Softened cream cheese
2 cups all-purpose flour
1/2 tsp. salt

Filling
1 medium onion, chopped (2/3 cup)
2 tbsp. butter
2 1/2 cups finely grated Swiss cheese (10 oz)
3 eggs
1 1/2 cups half and half
1/2 tsp salt
dash of pepper
dash of ground nutmeg

First, make the pastry. Preheat the oven to 350'. Grease 60 miniature muffin cups.

Combine the butter, cream cheese, flour and salt until well blended. Roll into balls and press into the prepared miniature muffin cups. Bake for 3-5 minutes.

**Continued on next page**

Next, make the filling. Saute' the onions in the butter until transparent.

Place a tsp. of the Swiss cheese in each pastry shell.

Blend the eggs, cream, salt, pepper and nutmeg. Mix in the onions. Placed 1 tsp. of the egg mixture over the cheese in each pastry shell, filling 2/3 full.

Bake in a 350' oven for 20 minutes or until set and lightly browned.

Yield: 60 miniature quiches

*This book is published by*
*Callawind Publications, $14.95, soft cover*

# Miniature BLT Sandwiches
## "Breakfast at Nine, Tea at Four"
### Favorite Recipes from
### Cape May's Mainstay Inn
### by Sue Carroll

8 slices firm white bread
6 strips bacon, cooked and crumbled
1/3 cup mayonnaise
Green leaf lettuce
4 plum tomatoes, thinly sliced

Using a 2" cutter, cut the bread into 24 rounds.

Blend the bacon with the mayonnaise and spread the mixture over the bread rounds. Place a piece of lettuce on each and top with a slice of tomato.

Yield: 24 open-faced sandwiches

*This book is published by*
*Callawind Publications, $14.95. softcover*

# Pineapple Kiwi Tea Sandwiches

*"A Year of Teas at the Elmwood Inn"*
*by Shelley and Bruce Richardson*

1 - 8 oz. package cream cheese, room temp
1/4 cup pineapple preserves
1 tbsp. mayonnaise
2 fresh kiwi, peeled and sliced thin
16 slices whole wheat bread

Remove crusts from bread and cut into small rounds. In medium bowl, mix together cream cheese, preserves, and mayonnaise. Spread evenly on top of each slice of bread. Top with a piece of kiwi.

Makes 32 open-faced sandwiches

# Rosy Beef Broth
# with Spinach
"Pomeroy House"
Yacolt, Washington

2 cups beef broth
1/2 cup cran-cherry juice
1 tsp. lemon juice
1/2 tsp. Worcestershire sauce
Dash hot pepper sauce
Salt and pepper to taste

Combine ingredients and simmer for 10 minutes.

Pour over fresh spinach leaves washed and cut into 1/4 inch strips. They use approximately 1/4 to 1/3 cups per bowl. Garnish with lemon slices.

Makes 4 servings

# Sun Dried Tomato Sandwiches

"Pomeroy House"
Yacolt, Washington

2/3 cup sun-dried tomatoes
1/4 cup chopped walnuts
8 oz. cream cheese, softened
1/4 cup freshly grated Parmesan cheese
1 clove garlic, minced
2 tbsp. fresh basil, chopped

Finely chopped tomatoes in a food processor, combine with remaining ingredients in a medium bowl. Spread filling on sour dough or cocktail bread. Garnish with parsley.

# Tomato Basil
# Tea Sandwiches

## "A Year of Teas at the Elmwood Inn"
## by Shelley and Bruce Richardson

16 slices white bread
23 slices Roma tomatoes
mayonnaise
Mixture of dried herbs
Small fresh basil leaves
Salt to taste

Remove crusts from bread and cut into small rounds. Mix the dried herbs, mayonnaise and salt together and spread thinly over each cut-out. Top each with a tomato slice and a small basil leaf.

Makes 32 open-faced sandwiches

# Cheery Cherry Sandwiches

*"Once Upon a Time"*
*Central Point, Oregon*

16 oz. Cream cheese
Chopped pecans, optional
Large jar maraschino cherries with some liquid

Soften cream cheese. Cut up cherries and add to cream cheese. Add enough cherry juice to make soft sandwich spread. Add pecans, if desired. Spread on white bread, trim crusts, and cut into desired shapes.

# Asparagus Roll-Ups

## "La Tea Da'

### Tillamook, Oregon

16 fresh asparagus spears
16 slices moist sandwich bread, crusts removed
1 pkg. (8oz.) cream cheese, softened
8 bacon strips, cooked and crumbled
2 tbsp. minced chives
1 green onion, chopped
1/2 cup grated Tillamook cheese
1/4 cup butter, melted
3 tbsp. grated Parmesan cheese

Place asparagus in a skillet with a small amount of water, cook until crisp-tender, about 6-8 minutes. Drain and set aside. Flatten bread with a rolling pin. Combine the cream cheese, cheddar, green onions, bacon and chives; spread 1 tbsp. on each slice of bread. Top with an asparagus spear. Roll up tightly; place seam side down on a greased baking sheet. Brush with butter and sprinkle with Parmesan cheese. Cut roll-ups in half. Bake at 400' for 10-12 minutes or until lightly browned.

Yield: 32 savories

# Bleu Cheese Crisps

## "Joyful Hearts Tea Room and Gift Shop"
### Corvallis, Oregon

4 oz. Bleu cheese
2 tbsp. dry minced onions
2 tbsp. butter or margarine
1 egg
1 pkg. cream cheese
Pie crust for 2 crust pie
Grated cheddar (optional)
Paprika (optional)

Beat bleu cheese, onion, butter, egg and cream cheese until fluffy. Cover and chill. Roll half of the pastry into a 12" x 8" rectangle. Spread half of the filling over half of the pastry. Fold dough over to make a 12" x 4" rectangle. Seal edges well, pressing out air bubbles.

Using a pastry wheel, cut into 1" squares. Place squares on un-greased sheet pan. Sprinkle lightly with cheddar and paprika, if desired. Repeat with a second half of the pastry and filling. Bake at 425' for 12-15 minutes, until puffy and browned.

# Curried Tuna Salad Sandwich

## "Joyful Hearts Tea Room and Gift Shop"

### Corvallis, Oregon

1 can (7 oz.) tuna, drained and flaked
1/4 cup chopped celery
2 tbsp. Raisins
2 tbsp. sliced green onions
1/4 tsp. lemon juice
1/4 - 1/2 tsp. curry powder
1/4 tsp. salt
Mini pita pockets or bread of choice

Combine tuna, celery, raisins and green onions in a bowl. In a small bowl, stir together the mayonnaise, lemon juice, curry powder and salt. Stir into tuna. Slice pita pockets in half or cut bread into finger sandwich size, and fill with curried chicken.

# Scones,

# Desserts

# and

# Toppings

# Nana's (Emma Roedde) Almond Cookies
### "Roedde House Museum"
### Vancouver, B.C., Canada

1 cup butter
2/3 cup white sugar
2 1/2 cups flour
1 egg
1 tsp. cream of tartar
1/2 tsp. baking soda
1 tbsp. boiling water
Blanched almonds

Cream together butter, sugar and eggs. Sift together dry ingredients, add to mixture. Roll into balls, and roll in white sugar. Press 1/2 blanched almond onto tops of cookies. Bake at 325' for 15 minutes. Watch for color.

# Buckingham Palace Shortbread

"Afternoon Tea Serenade"
Recipes from Famous Tea Rooms
Classical Chamber Music
by Sharon O'Connor

2 cups unsalted butter at room temperature
2/3 cups granulated sugar
4 cups pastry flour
1 1/3 cups cornstarch
Superfine sugar for sprinkling

In a large bowl, cream the butter and sugar together until pale and fluffy. In a medium bowl, stir the flour and cornstarch together. Gently stir the flour mixture into the butter mixture until it forms a soft dough. Cover the dough with plastic wrap and refrigerate for about 15 minutes, or until form.

Preheat the oven to 325'. Dust the dough lightly with flour and roll it out to 3/4" thick square or rectangle on a sheet of parchment paper. Transfer the parchment paper and dough to a baking sheet. Bake in the center of the pre-heated oven for 30-40 minute, or until lightly golden and firm to the touch. Remove from the oven and sprinkle the shortbread generously with the superfine sugar. While still warm, use a paring knife to cut the shortbread into 48 pieces.

# Bavarian Apple Tarts
### "Tea Events"
### Bend, Oregon

Crust:
1/2 cup butter
1/3 cup sugar
1/2 tsp. vanilla
1 cup unbleached flour

Cream butter, vanilla and sugar together and with a pastry cutter, blend in the flour. The dough will be crumbly. Press into bottom and up sides of a greased tart pan (a spring form pan may be substituted for the tart pan if necessary).

Filling:
8 oz. pkg. cream cheese softened
1/4 cup sugar
1 egg, slightly beaten
1/2 tsp. vanilla

Combine softened cream cheese and sugar. Mix well. Add the beaten egg and vanilla. Mix well and pour into the pastry - lined pan.

**Continued on next page**

Topping:
1/3 cup sugar
1/2 tsp. cinnamon
1/4 tsp. nutmeg
pinch of salt
4 large apples, peeled and sliced thinly
1/2 cup slivered almonds (optional)

Combine the sugar, salt, cinnamon and nutmeg. Toss the sugar mixture with the slices of apples in a large bowl. Let this stand for at least 15 minutes. Arrange the apples over the cream cheese layer and sprinkle with the almonds, as desired.

*From the Tea Events*
*Recipe Book*

# Almond Torte Bars

Bottom layer:
2 1/2 cups yellow cake mix
1 egg
1/4 cup melted butter
1 tsp. almond extract

Top layer:
6 oz. softened cream cheese
2 eggs
2 1/2 cups powdered sugar

1/2 cup slivered almonds

Mix bottom layer ingredients and spread across the bottom of a greased 9 x 13 pan. The dough is stick so use the bottom of a measuring cup to flatten into the pan.

For the top layer, blend cream cheese and eggs and mix in the powdered sugar. Pour this over the bottom layer and then top with the almonds. Bake at 350' for about 30 minutes our until golden brown. Remove from oven and sprinkle with powdered sugar.

# Carrot Raisin Loaf
## "Applewood"
### North Delta, B.C., Canada

1 1/3 cups water
1 1/2 cups sugar
1 cup grated carrots
1 cup raisins
5 tsp. margarine or butter
1 tsp. clove
1 tsp. cinnamon
1 tsp. nutmeg

Put the above ingredients in a saucepan
and boil for 5 minutes. Cool.

When ingredients are cool, add the following:

2 cups flour
1 egg
1 tsp. baking soda
1 tsp. baking powder

Mix together until blended. Pour into greased
loaf pan and bake at 350' for 1 hour.

# Chocolate Chip Oatmeal Cookies

*"London Heritage Farm"*
*Richmond, B.C., Canada*

1/2 cup butter
3/4 cups brown sugar
3/4 cup white sugar
1 tsp. vanilla
1 tsp. hot water
1 egg
1 1/2 cups flour
1 tsp. salt
1 tsp. baking soda
2 cups chocolate chips
2 cups oatmeal

Preheat oven to 375'. Cream butter and sugars. Add vanilla, hot water and eggs. Add flour, salt and baking soda then mix in chocolate chips and oatmeal. Bake for approximately 10 minutes.

# Coffee Bars
## "London Heritage Farm"
## Richmond, B.C., Canada

1/2 cup butter
1 cup brown sugar
1/2 cup hot coffee
1 1/2 cups flour
1/2 tsp. baking soda
1/2 tsp. baking powder
1 tsp. cinnamon
1 egg
1/4 cup coconut
1/2 cup raisins

Glaze: 1 cup powdered sugar, 2 tbsp. milk
and1/2 tsp vanilla

Mix together batter ingredients. Bake in flat 16x11x1 inch pan at 350' for 20 to 25 minutes. Combine powdered sugar, milk and vanilla. Pour over mixture while hot.

Cool and cut into 1 inch bars.

# Cookie Tarts
## "Tea Events"
### Bend, Oregon

Cookie tarts are easy and always get rave reviews! Use your favorite sugar cookie recipe or your favorite peanut butter cookie recipe. In a pinch you can even use pre-packaged cookie dough from the grocery store.

**Tart Shells:**

Tart shells are made by pressing the cookie dough into the tart pan. Do not grease the pan. Bake in a 350' oven for 8 minutes. take the pan out and press the center of the tart down using the back of a spoon to make an indentation. Return to the oven for 2 minutes. Allow the tarts to cook and remove from the pan.

**Fillling:**

Puddings such as chocolate or banana cream make easy and creamy fillings. Make the pudding as listed on the back of the box. Place the pudding in a piping bag and pipe into tart shells. Garnish with a bit of whipped cream and a few chocolate shavings or a bit of banana and a zest of lemon curl.

Jams are also good fillings. Mix 1/4 cup of jam with 1 cup of fresh whipped cream. Fold the mixture together and pipe into shells. Add sliced strawberries and sprinkle with cinnamon.

**Also try lemon curd recipe on next page** ☞

# Lemon Curd

## "KJ's Kitchen and Catering"
### Albany, Oregon

2 large eggs plus 2 large egg yolks.
3/4 cup sugar
2/3 cup fresh lemon juice (about 3 lemons)
2 tsp. grated lemon peel
1/3 cup butter, chilled and cut into small pieces
Few grains of salt

In a heavy sauce pan, whisk eggs and yolks together. Add sugar, lemon juice and peel. Sprinkle in salt and add butter pieces.

Cook over low heat, stirring constantly with a wooden spoon until it thickens enough to coat the back of the spoon, about 8 minutes. Don't let the mixture boil.

Strain and pour into a heat proof glass and cover with plastic wrap. Refrigerate for at least 4 hours before serving.

Makes about 1 1/2 cups

# Country Scones
# with Devonshire Cream

"The Rose of Gig Harbor
Bed & Breakfast and Tea Room"
Gig Harbor, Washington

1 egg
buttermilk, to make 1 cup when combined with egg
2 cups flour
1/4 cup sugar
2 1/2 tsp. baking powder
1/2 tsp. salt
6 tbsp. cold, firm butter
1/2 cup raisins or dried fruit such as cranberries,
strawberries or blueberries
1/2 cup white baking chips (morsels)
Devonshire cream (recipe to follow)

Preheat oven to 400'. In a one cup measure, slightly beat egg. Add buttermilk to fill. Set aside. In a large bowl, sift flour, sugar, baking powder and salt. Using a pastry blender, cut in butter until mixture is crumbly. Toss in raisins (or fruit) and baking chips. Add buttermilk mixture and stir just until dough clings together. Do not overmix! On ungreased baking sheet, drop dough by ¼ cupfuls. Bake for 12-15 minutes, or until lightly browned.

Serve with Devonshire Cream.

# Devonshire Cream

1-3 oz. package of cream cheese, room temperature
1 tbsp. confectioners sugar
1/2 tsp. vanilla
1/3 cup whipping cream (may use up to 1/2 cup)

In a small bowl, beat together cream cheese, confectioners sugar and vanilla until fluffy. Add whipping cream and beat just until spreading consistency. Do not over beat.

Makes about 1 cup

# Currant Scones
## "A Touch of Elegance"
### St. John, Washington

3 cups flour
1/4 cup sugar
1 tbsp. baking powder
1/2 tsp. baking soda
1/2 tsp. Salt
3/4 cups cold butter
1 cup buttermilk
2/3 cups currants
2 tbsp. whipping cream

Combine first five ingredients mixing well. Cut in butter until mixture resembles coarse meal. Add buttermilk and currants stirring until dry ingredients are moist. Shape dough into a ball and place on lightly floured surface. Roll dough to 1/2 inch thick and cut with a 2" heart shaped cutter. Place scones on an ungreased baking sheet. Brush with whipping cream. Bake at 400' for 12-15 minutes.

Makes 2 dozen

# Date/Walnut Scones
### "Vintage Inn B & B"
### Vancouver, Washington

1 1/3 cups cake flour
3 tbsp. sugar
2 tsp. baking powder
1/8 tsp. salt
3 tbsp. cold unsalted butter cut into small pieces
1/2 cup chopped dates
1/4 cup chopped walnuts
1/3 cup buttermilk
1/2 tsp. vanilla

Preheat oven to 425'. Line a baking sheet with wax paper. In a medium bowl, combine the flour, sugar, baking powder and salt. Cut in the butter until the mixture resembles fine breadcrumbs. Stir in the dates and walnuts. In a small bowl, mix the buttermilk and vanilla. Add to dry ingredients and stir with a fork just until the dough comes together. Turn the dough out onto a lightly floured surface and knead twice. Pat the dough into a round and cut into wedges. Set on prepared baking sheet and bake for 12 minutes or until a pale golden color. Cool on wire rack.

Makes 8

# Devonshire Cream, Mock
### "All the Tea in China"
### by Yvonne Wrightman

1 cup heavy whipping cream
4 oz. cream cheese
Dash vanilla

In a food processor or blender, blend all the ingredients until the cream cheese has completely disappeared and the mixture is thickened. Great with scones or gingerbread.

Makes 1 1/2 cups

This book can still be obtained at the original price from:
Printwest Communications Ltd.
1150 Eighth Avenue
Regina, Saskatchewan, Canada S4R 1C9

# Eggnog Holiday Bread
## "The Twelve Days of Christmas"
### by Emily Barnes

3 cups flour
3/4 cups sugar
1 tbsp. baking powder
1 tsp. salt
1/2 tsp. nutmeg
1 1/2 cups dairy eggnog
1 egg, beaten
1/4 cup butter, melted
3/4 cup pecans, chopped
3/4 cups candied fruit

In a large bowl, sift together flour, sugar, baking powder, salt and nutmeg. In a separate bowl, mix eggnog, egg and butter, Add wet ingredients to dry, stirring well. Add pecans and fruit. Bake in greased loaf pan at 350' for 60 to 70 minutes. Cool on wire rack.

# Fancy Fruit Dip
## The Rose of Gig Harbor
## Bed & Breakfast and Tea Room
## Gig Harbor, Washington

1 - 8 oz. jar Marshmallow Cream
1 - 8 oz. cream cheese softened
1/4 cup confectioners sugar (sifted)

Allow cream cheese to come to room temperature. Whip until fluffy, add marshmallow cream, and slowly mix in sugar until well blended. Store in refrigerator...it will remain dipping consistency.

This is lovely served in the center of a sliced cantaloupe surrounded by such fruits as pineapple, strawberries and cubed cantaloupe.

# Roedde House
# Gingerbread Cookies
### "Roedde House Museum"
### Vancouver, B.C., Canada

1 cup margarine or butter
2 cups brown sugar
2 eggs
4 tbsp. Golden Syrup
3 1/2 cups flour
1 tsp. cinnamon
6 tsp. powdered ginger
1 tsp. baking soda

Cream together butter and sugar, add eggs, then syrup.
Add dry ingredients. Put in refrigerator to firm up for 1/2
hour. Roll into balls and flatten with a fork. Bake at 375'
12-15 minutes.

# *Forgotten Torte*
## *Janice Palmquist at Deepwood Estate*
## *Salem, Oregon*

About 2 hours before the overnight baking, place 6 egg whites in a large mixing bowl and let them stand at room temperature. Preheat the oven to 450' and butter only the bottom of a 9" tube pan with a removable bottom. Add 1/2 tsp. cream of tartar and 1/4 tsp. salt to the egg whites. Beat with a mixer at medium speed until the egg whites are foamy. Gradually add 1 1/2 cups of sugar, a little at a time, beating well after each addition. Add 1 tsp. vanilla extract, 1/8 tsp. almond extract and a few drops of pink food coloring. Continue beating the mixture until the meringue forms stiff glossy peaks. Spread the mixture evenly in the tube pan and place the pan in the oven. Turn the oven off and leave the pan in the oven overnight.

In the morning, loosen the edge of the torte with a sharp knife and turn the torte over onto a serving platter. The cake will settle a bit. To serve, frost the cake with whipped cream made from 1 cup of whipping cream. Garnish with fresh berries or raspberry sauce.

**See next page for sauce recipe.**

# Raspberry Sauce for Torte

10 oz. package of frozen raspberries,
thawed and drained,
reserving the juice
1/4 cup sugar
2 tbsp. cornstarch
1-2 tbsp. orange or raspberry
flavored liqueur, if desired

Add water to the reserved raspberry juice to make 1 1/4 cups of liquid. Mix sugar with the cornstarch in a 1 quart saucepan, stirring in the juice and raspberries. Heat to a boil over medium heat. Boil and stir for 1 minute, smashing the berries as much as possible. Strain if you desire a syrup or leave unstrained with berry pulp in your sauce. Stir in the liqueur and let cool. You can put the finished sauce in a squeeze bottle with a small end cut and drizzle it over the slice of torte with a puddle to one side. If the consistency isn't thin enough to drizzle, you can add a little water. Put the sauce on just before serving as it will bleed into the whipped cream.

*Recipe is from Janice's Cookbook*
*"Deepwood Delights - Secrets*
*for Enjoyable Teas"*

# Golden Nuggets
## "Blue Angel"
### Milwaukie, Oregon

1 cup butter
6 heaping tbsp. powdered sugar
2 cups cake flour
1 tsp. vanilla
1 cup walnuts

Allow butter to soften, then cream with the sugar. Add flour, vanilla and nuts. Roll into walnut sized balls and bake on unbuttered sheet pan at 350' for about 12 minutes. Cool and dust with powdered sugar.

# Nectarberry Curd
## *"A La Fontaine"*
### *Albany, Oregon*

4 egg yolks at room temperature
1/2 cup granulated sugar
(they use whole cane)
Grated lemon zest
1/2 cup fresh nectarberry juice

In a double boiler, whisk egg yolks and sugar. Add lemon zest and juice. Set over simmering water, whisking constantly until thickened. Approximately 10 minutes. Remove from heat. Pour into glass containers to chill. Cover with plastic wrap. Last several days.

Makes one cup

*This is their house specialty!*

# Lavender Shortbread
### "Tracy Hill"
### Bend, Oregon

1 1/2 cups butter at room temperature
2/3 cup sugar
2 tbsp. very finely chopped lavender-
(fresh or dried)
1 tbsp. chopped fresh spearmint
2 1/2 cups flour
1/2 cup cornstarch
1/4 tsp. salt

Preheat oven to 325'. Cover bottoms of two baking sheets with parchment or brown paper. In a large bowl, cream together the butter, sugar, lavender and spearmint with an electric mixer. Mix until light and fluffy, about 3 minutes. Add flour, cornstarch and salt and beat until incorporated. Divide dough in half. Flatten into squares and wrap in plastic. Chill until firm.

On a floured board, roll or pat out each square to a thickness of 1/2 inch. Cut the dough into 1 1/2 inch squares or rounds. Transfer to baking sheet, spacing about 1 inch apart. Prick each cookie several times with a fork. Bake 20-25 minutes until pale golden (do not brown). Cool slightly, then transfer to a rack. Sprinkle with Lavender Powdered Sugar.

Makes about 4 dozen.

**Continued**

# Lavender Powdered Sugar

Put 4 or 5 sprigs of lavender flowers in a sealed jar with powdered sugar overnight. Sift before using. Adds a lovely flavor to butter cream frosting or other recipes using powdered sugar.

This recipe is from the Tracy Hill Recipe Collection and Anita says that, "This is her absolute favorite recipe! You just might want to make a double batch!"

# Lavender Scones
### "Tea and Tomes"
### Newport, Oregon

2 cups flour
1 tbsp. baking powder
4 tbsp. butter
1/4 cup sugar
2 tsp. fresh lavender florets
or 1 tsp. dried Culinary lavender
2/3 cups milk, plus extra for glazing

Preheat oven to 425'. Grease and flour a large baking sheet. Sift the flour and baking powder together in a large mixing bowl. Rub in the butter until the mixture resembles fine bread crumbs. Stir in the sugar and lavender, reserving a pinch to sprinkle on top of the scones before baking. Add enough milk to make a soft, sticky dough, then turn it out on a well-floured surface. Shape the dough into a round about one inch thick. Using a round pastry cutter, stamp out 12 scones. Place the scones on the prepared baking sheet, brush the tops with a little milk, and sprinkle on the reserved chopped lavender. Bake in a preheated oven for 10-12 minutes until golden.

Serve with warm cream and jam.

Makes 12

# Overnight Orange Cookies

### "London Heritage Farm"
### Richmond, B.C., Canada

1/2 cup butter
1 cup sugar
1 egg
1 tsp. vanilla
1/3 cup orange or lemon juice
1 tbsp. orange rind

3 cups flour
1 tsp. baking powder
1 tsp. salt

Cream butter and sugar, add egg and vanilla. Add orange or lemon juice and rind. Add flour, baking powder and salt.

Divide into two rolls; form each into log shape. Wrap in wax paper and chill overnight. Slice, not too thin. Bake on greased cookie sheet in 350' oven for about 15 minutes.

If you prefer, you can drop by teaspoonful onto cookie sheet without chilling

# Lemon Sour Cream Pound Cake
### "Just Pretend"
### Port Townsend, Washington

3 cups all-purpose flour
1/2 tsp. baking powder
1/4 tsp. baking soda
1/2 tsp. salt
1 cup (2 sticks) unsalted butter at room temperature
3 cups sugar
6 eggs at room temperature
1 tsp. vanilla extract
Grated zest of 2 lemons
1 cup sour cream, at room temperature

Position a rack in the center of the oven and preheat to 325'. Butter and flour a 10" bun pan, and tap out excess flour. Sift the flour, baking powder, baking soda and salt together; set aside. Beat the butter and sugar in a large bowl with a hand held electric mixer on high speed until light and fluffy, about 3 minutes. Beat in the eggs, one at a time, then vanilla and zest. On low speed, add the flour in 3 additions, alternating with 2 additions of the sour cream, beginning and ending with flour. Beat until smooth, scraping down the sides of the bowl often with a rubber spatula. Spread evenly in the pan. Bake until a wooden skewer inserted in the center of the cake comes out clean, about 1 hour and 15 minutes. Drizzle with syrup – **recipe to follow on next page.**

# Lemon Syrup:

Zest of lemon
1 cup fresh lemon juice
1/4 cup water
2/3 cup sugar

Bring the lemon juice, zest, water and sugar to a boil over high heat and cook until it is reduced to 1/2 cup, about 15 minutes. Allow the syrup to cool before drizzling onto the cake.

Transfer the cake to a wire rack and cool for 10 minutes. Drizzle half the syrup over the cake. Invert onto the rack and brush with remaining syrup. Cool completely.

Makes 12 servings

# Raspberry Meringue Squares

*"Afternoon Tea Serenade"*
*Recipes from Famous Tea Rooms*
*Classical Chamber Music*
*by Sharon O'Connor*

2 1/2 cups unbleached all-purpose flour
2 cups sugar
1 cup butter at room temperature
2 egg yolks
3/4 cups raspberry jam
4 egg whites
1 1/2 cups blanched almonds, chopped

Preheat the oven to 350'. Butter a 10 x 15 inch jelly roll pan. In a large bowl, stir the flour, 1 1/2 cups of the sugar, the butter, and egg yolks together until well blended. Press the dough into the prepared pan, prick all over with a fork, and bake in the preheated oven for 15 to 20 minutes, or until golden. Remove from the oven, but leave the oven on.

Spread the raspberry jam over the baked layer. In a large bowl, beat the egg whites until foamy, then gradually beat in the remaining 1/2 cup sugar and continue to beat until stiff, glossy peaks form. Fold in the almonds. Spread the meringue over the jam. Return the pan to the oven and bake for 25 minutes, or until lightly browned. Let cool and cut into 2" squares.

Makes 35 - 2" squares

# Strawberry Sorbet
### *"A Year of Teas at the Elmwood Inn"*
### *by Shelley and Bruce Richardson*

1 1/2 cups iced cold waster
1/4 cup powdered sugar
2 - 10 oz. Packages frozen strawberries in
syrup, thawed
Fresh strawberries
Fresh mint leaves

Puree water, sugar and thawed strawberries in a blender.
Pour mixture into a sorbet maker and freeze until almost
firm. Stir regularly. Dip out into another container with
lid. Freeze until ready to serve. Form small sorbet balls
with an ice-cream scoop. Garnish with fresh strawberries
and mint.

Serves 12

# Rhubarb

# Upside-Down Cake
### "Applewood"
### North Delta, B.C., Canada

2/3 cup boiling water
1/2 cup quick cooking oats
2 tbsp. margarine or butter
1/3 cup granulated sugar
2 cups diced rhubarb
1 cup all purpose flour
1 tsp. baking powder
1/4 tsp. baking soda
1/2 tsp. cinnamon
1/4 tsp. salt
2/3 cups granulated sugar
1/2 cup packed brown sugar
1/4 cup cooking oil
1 egg

In a medium bowl, pour the boiling water over the rolled oats, cover and let stand for 20 minutes.

Meanwhile, place the margarine or butter in an 8 x 8 baking pan and heat in a 350' oven for about 2 minutes or until melted. Stir in the 1/3 cup granulated sugar. Sprinkle the rhubarb over the sugar and set aside.

In a medium bowl, stir together the flour, baking powder, baking soda, cinnamon and salt. Set Aside. In a large mixing bowl, combine the 2/3 cups granulated sugar, brown sugar, oil and egg. Beat until combined. Add the oat mixture and beat well. Add the flour mixture to the oat mixture, beating just until combined.

### Continued on next page

Carefully pour the cake batter atop the rhubarb mixture. Bake in a 350' oven for about 50 minutes or until a tooth-pick inserted near the centre comes out clean. Cool on a rack for 5 minutes. Run a knife along sides to loosen and invert onto a serving plate. Serve warm.

Serves 9

* If you are using frozen rhubarb, measure 2 cups of frozen sliced rhubarb. Thaw slightly and chop. Return to bowl and thaw completely before using.

# Hazelnut Meringues with Raspberries and Cream

"Once Upon a Time"
Central Point, Oregon

4 egg whites
1/2 tsp. white vinegar
1 1/4 cups plus 1 tsp. sugar
1 cup hazelnuts, toasted and grould
2 cups whipping cream (not ultra pasteurized)
1 tbsp. powdered sugar
2 1/2 cups fresh raspberries
(Teri likes to use frozen as they turn the
cream a lovely pink and they cost less.
The fresh do not turn the cream pink)

Beat egg whites until stiff, but not dry. When whites form soft peaks, add vinegar and continue beating until stiff. Fold sugar into whites, then fold in ground nuts. Divide the batter into two lightly greased 8" cake pans and bake for 30 minutes at 375'. Remove meringues from pans and immediately cool. Whip cream with powdered sugar until stiff peaks form. Fold in raspberries. Spread whipped cream and raspberry mixture on top of meringue and place the other meringue on top. Dust with powdered sugar.

Teri says that "This is an easy dessert that looks expensive and it is just delicious. The meringue tastes like wonderful cookies".

# English Trifle
## "Once Upon a Time"
### Central Point, Oregon

2 (8 or 9") white cake layers, baked and cooled
2 pints fresh strawberries
1/4 cup white sugar
1 pint fresh blueberries
2 bananas
1/4 cup orange juice
1 (3.5 oz.) package instant vanilla pudding mix
2 cup milk
2 cup heavy whipping cream
1/4 cup blanched slivered almonds
12 maraschino cherries

1) Slice strawberries and sprinkle them with sugar. Cut the bananas into slices and toss with the orange juice. Combine pudding mix with milk and mix until smooth. Cut the cake into 1" cubes.

2) Use half the cake cubes to line the bottom of a large glass bowl. Layer half of the strawberries followed by half of the blueberries, then half of the bananas. Spread half of the pudding over the fruit. Repeat layers in the same order.

3) In a medium bowl, whip the cream to stiff peaks and spread over the top of the trifle. Garnish with maraschino cherries and slivered almonds.

# Chewy Chocolate Cookies
## "Once Upon a Time"
### Central Point, Oregon

1 1/4 cups butter, softened
2 cups white sugar
2 eggs
2 tsp. vanilla extract
2 cups all-purpose flour
3/4 cups unsweetened cocoa powder
2 tsp. baking soda
1/2 tsp. salt
2 cups semi-sweet chocolate chips

Preheat oven to 350'F (180' C)

In a large mixer bowl, cream butter and sugar until light and fluffy. Add eggs and vanilla; beat well.

Sift together flour, cocoa, baking soda and salt; gradually blend into creamed mixture, using low speed on mixer. Stir in chocolate chips with a wooden spoon. Drop by teaspoonfuls onto un-greased cookie sheets. Bake 8-9 minutes. DO NOT over-bake!. Cookies will be soft. They will puff while baking and flatten while cooling. Cool slightly on cookie sheet, remove from sheet onto wire rack to cool completely.

# Lemon Curd
## "Once Upon a Time"
### Central Point, Oregon

Grated rind and juice of 3 lemons
3 eggs
4 oz. Butter
1 cup sugar

Wash the lemons and grind the rind finely. Place the lemon juice, grated rind, butter and sugar in a bowl and set over a saucepan of hot water. Stir until butter has melted and sugar dissolves. Beat the eggs in a separate bowl and add slowly to the lemon mixture, stirring steadily. Put all into a saucepan and cook, stirring occasionally, until sauce thickens.

# "Devonshire" Cream
## "Once Upon a Time"
### Central Point, Oregon

1/2 cup heavy cream
2 tbsp. confectioner's sugar
1/2 cup sour cream

In a chilled bowl, beat cream until medium-stiff peaks form, adding sugar during the last few minutes of beating. Fold in the sour cream and blend.

Spreads for cookies and cakes include jellies,

jams and marmalade.

# Strawberry Butter
### "Once Upon a Time"
### Central Point, Oregon

3/4 cups frozen strawberries, thawed and drained
1 cup butter, softened
3 tbsp. confectioners' sugar

Mix ingredients in blender until smooth. Refrigerate.

Makes about 2 cups

OR

3/4 cups fresh strawberries, cleaned and hulled
1/2 cup (1 stick) butter, softened
1/4 cup confectioners' sugar

Puree strawberries in blender or mixer. Blend in butter and sugar until smooth, fluffy and bright pink. Serve.

# Raspberry Butter
### "Once Upon a Time"
### Central Point, Oregon

8 oz. Cream cheese, softened
1/2 pound cold butter or margarine
1 pound confectioners' sugar
1/2 cup fresh raspberries

To make raspberry butter, microwave berries for 1 minute. Chill. Whip cream cheese and butter until fluffy. Add raspberries and powdered sugar. Mix until blended. Refrigerate until ready to serve.

Leftover raspberry butter freezes well.

# Lemon Curd Tarts

## "Leach Botanical Gardens"
## Portland, Oregon

### Curd

3 eggs
5 tbsp. melted butter
1 cup white sugar
1/2 lemon juice (juice of 2 lemons)
Zest from two lemons

### Tart

1 cup flour
1 cube butter
4 oz. cream cheese

Beat the eggs slightly, then beat into melted butter. Stir in sugar and beat well. Add lemon juice and rind (zest) gradually. Cook over simmering water until thickened, stirring constantly, about 15 minutes. Cool and refrigerate. Will last about 1 week.

Blend tart ingredients with a pastry knife until cornmeal size, then knead a few times. Chill before rolling. Either roll or pinch off a small amount and form in small muffin tins that are well greased. With knife trim each pastry shell even with the top of the pan. With fork, prick the bottom of each tart shell. **Very important.** Bake 10-12 minutes until golden brown. Turn shells out of pan onto wire rack to cool. Fill with lemon curd. Enjoy!

# Tea Truffles

## "MS Maasdam"

### Executive Chef - Marcus Jenni

14.1 ounces whole milk
1.1 ounces tea
12.3 ounces heavy cream
35.3 ounces Swiss Line Chocolate Coins Dark
5.3 ounces butter
252 pieces 1" semisweet truffle shells

## Tea Ganache

Bring milk to boil. Add tea leaves and let infuse for approximately 1/2 hour. Remove tea leaves from milk, strain milk and combine with heavy cream. Bring heavy cream-milk mixture to a boil. Add Carma Swiss Line Couverture Dark Coins. Add softened butter and allow to cool to 79'. Fill into chocolate truffle shells. Let set overnight. Seal chocolate shells with tempered couverture. Dip filled truffle shells into tempered couverture and roll them on a wire rack.

Makes 252 Tea Truffles! Go for it!

# Almond Cookies

## "MS Massdam"

### Executive Chef Marcus Jenni

2 lb. plus 2oz butter
3 lb. plus 4oz. Sugar
5 whole eggs
2 lb. plus 12oz. Flour
2 lb. plus 12oz. Sliced almonds
3 oz. Vanilla flavor

Mix butter and sugar. Add eggs and vanilla flavor then add flour and almonds. *Do not over-mix!*

Make rolls of 1/2 inch in diameter and chill overnight. Cut into thin slices and sprinkle with sugar. Bake at 350' for abut 10 minutes or until golden brown.

When they are done, curl up by a large window with a cup of tea and some cookies and imagine you are on a cruise ship. Imagination is a wonderful thing!

# Lavender Flower Cookies

## "Leach Botanical Garden"

## Portland, Oregon

1/2 cup butter (1 cube)
1/2 cup margarine (1 cube)
1 - 1/2 cups granulated sugar
1 tsp. baking soda
Pinch of salt
2 tsp. cream of tartar
1/2 cup organic lavender blossoms,
stems and leaves removed
2 eggs, beaten
2 - 3/4 cups all-purpose flour

Cream together butter, margarine and sugar. Add soda, salt, cream of tartar and stir in lavender blossoms. Add beaten eggs and flour. Mix, then chill dough at least 4 hours. Roll into 3/4 inch balls and roll in granulated sugar, Or, the dough may be rolled out and cut in shapes with a cookie cutter. Bake at 400' for 5 to 8 minutes.

Makes 5 to 6 dozen cookies

# *Index*

# Recipes Index

## Beverages

Ginger Lemonade . . . . . . . . . . .   149
Lemonade Tea . . . . . . . . . . . .   150
Tea Recipes . . . . . . . . . . . . .   152
Zesty Butterscotch Tea . . . . . . . . .   151

## Sandwiches, Savories & Soups

Asparagus Rolls . . . . . . . . . . .   170
Bell Pepper Cheddar Chowder . . . . . . .   155
Bleu Cheese Crisps . . . . . . . . . .   171
Cheery Cherry Sandwiches . . . . . . . .   169
Cheese & Carrot Tea Sandwiches . . . . . .   156
Chicken Salad . . . . . . . . . . . .   157
Chicken Salad Florentine Sandwich . . . . .   158
Crispies . . . . . . . . . . . . . .   159
Cucumber and Roquefort Cheese Sandwiches . . . .   160
Curried Tuna Salad Sandwiches . . . . . .   172
Deviled Ham and Gherkins . . . . . . . .   161
Miniature BLT Sandwiches . . . . . . . .   164
Miniature Quiches. . . . . . . . . . .   162
Pineapple Kiwi Tea Sandwiches . . . . . .   165
Rosy Beef Broth w/spinach . . . . . . . .   166
Sandwiches, Favorite . . . . . . . . . .   154
Sun Dried Tomato Sandwiches. . . . . . .   167
Tomato Basil Tea Sandwiches . . . . . . .   168

# Recipes Index

## Scones, Desserts & Toppings

Almond Cookies . . . . . . . . . . . . . . 174
Almond Cookies . . . . . . . . . . . . . . 215
Almond Torte Bars . . . . . . . . . . . . 178
Bavarian Apple Tarts . . . . . . . . . . . 176
Carrot Raisin Loaf . . . . . . . . . . . . 179
Chewy Chocolate Cookies . . . . . . . . . 208
Chocolate Chip Oatmeal Cookies . . . . . . 180
Coffee Bars . . . . . . . . . . . . . . . 181
Cookie Tarts . . . . . . . . . . . . . . 182
Date/Walnut Scone . . . . . . . . . . . . 187
Devonshire Cream . . . . . . . . . . . . 185
Devonshire Cream . . . . . . . . . . . . 210
Devonshire Cream, Mock . . . . . . . . . 188
Eggnog Holiday Bread . . . . . . . . . . 189
English Trifle . . . . . . . . . . . . . 207
Fancy Fruit Dip . . . . . . . . . . . . . 190
Forgotten Torte . . . . . . . . . . . . . 192
Gingerbread Cookies . . . . . . . . . . . 191
Golden Nuggets . . . . . . . . . . . . . 194
Hazelnut Meringues w/Raspberries & Cream . . . 206
Lavender Flower Cookies . . . . . . . . . 216
Lavender Powdered Sugar . . . . . . . . . 197
Lemon Curd . . . . . . . . . . . . . . . 183
Lemon Curd . . . . . . . . . . . . . . . 209
Lemon Curd Tarts . . . . . . . . . . . . 213
Lemon Sour Cream Pound Cake . . . . . . . 200
Lemon Syrup . . . . . . . . . . . . . . 201
Nectarberry Curd . . . . . . . . . . . . 195
Overnight Orange Cookies . . . . . . . . . 199
Raspberry Butter . . . . . . . . . . . . 212
Raspberry Meringue Squares . . . . . . . . 202
Raspberry Sauce for Torte . . . . . . . . 193
Rhubarb Upside-Down Cake . . . . . . . . 204
Scones, Country . . . . . . . . . . . . . 184
Scones, Currant . . . . . . . . . . . . . 186
Scones, Lavender . . . . . . . . . . . . 198
Shortbread, Buckingham Palace . . . . . . . 175
Shortbread, Lavender . . . . . . . . . . . 196
Strawberry Butter . . . . . . . . . . . . 211
Strawberry Sorbet . . . . . . . . . . . . 203
Tea Truffles . . . . . . . . . . . . . . 214

# *Tea Rooms Index - Oregon*
## *Alphabetical Listing*
*(City Listing on page 225)*

| | | |
|---|---|---|
| A La Fontaine | *Albany* | 16 |
| Afternoon Delight | *Roseburg* | 17 |
| Afternoon Tea by Stephanie | *Canby* | 18 |
| Albertina's | *Portland* | 19 |
| Althea's Tea Room | *Dallas* | 20 |
| Ashland Springs Hotel | *Ashland* | 21 |
| | | |
| Blue Angel Heavenly Delectables | *Milwaukee* | 22 |
| Butteville General Store | *Aurora* | 23 |
| | | |
| Campbell House Inn | *Eugene* | 24 |
| Columbia Gorge Hotel | *Hood River* | 25 |
| | | |
| Deepwood Estate | *Salem* | 26 |
| | | |
| Eve's Garden Café & Tea Room | *Applegate* | 27 |
| | | |
| Flinn's Tea Room | *Albany* | 28 |
| | | |
| Gordon House | *Silverton* | 29 |
| | | |
| Heathman Hotel Restaurant | *Portland* | 30 |
| | | |
| In Good Taste | *Portland* | 31 |
| | | |
| Joyful Hearts Tea Room | *Corvallis* | 32 |
| Julia's Tea Parlor | *Salem* | 33 |
| | | |
| Kashin-Tei Tea House | *Portland* | 34 |
| KJ's Tea House | *Albany* | 35 |
| | | |
| La Tea Da Tea Room | *Tillamook* | 36 |
| Lady Di's Store & Tea Room | *Lake Oswego* | 37 |
| Lavender Tea House | *Sherwood* | 38 |
| Leach Botanical Garden | *Portland* | 39 |

# Tea Rooms Index - Oregon
## Alphabetical Listing
### (City Listing on page 225)

| | | |
|---|---|---|
| Mon Ami | Florence | 40 |
| Mrs. B's Special Teas | Lebanon | 41 |
| | | |
| Nauna's Tea Room | Salem | 42 |
| Newell House Museum | St. Paul | 43 |
| | | |
| Once Upon a Time | Central Point | 44 |
| Oregon Tea Garden | Silverton | 45 |
| | | |
| Primrose Tea Room | McMinnville | 46 |
| | | |
| Rose's Tea Room | Gresham | 47 |
| Ruthie B's | Springfield | 48 |
| | | |
| Savoure | Eugene | 49 |
| Shelton-McMurphey-Johnson House | Eugene | 50 |
| Sister Act Party Specialists | Corvallis | 51 |
| | | |
| Tea & Tomes, Ltd. | Newport | 52 |
| Tea Cosy, The | Bandon | 53 |
| Tea Events | Bend | 54 |
| Tea Zone | Portland | 55 |
| Tracy Hill Home & Garden | Bend | 56 |
| Tudor Rose Tea Room | Salem | 57 |
| | | |
| Wakai Tea Room | Portland | 58 |
| Wild Rose Tea Room, The | Redmond | 59 |

# Tea Rooms Index - Washington
## Alphabetical Listing
### (City Listing on page 228)

| | | |
|---|---|---|
| A Touch of Elegance | *St. John* | 62 |
| Abbey Garden Tea Room | *Bellingham* | 63 |
| All About Tea | | 64 |
| Althea's Tea Lounge | *Mount Vernon* | 65 |
| Anna's Tea Room | *Coupeville* | 66 |
| Attic Secrets Tea Room | *Marysville* | 67 |
| Brambleberry Cottage Tea Shoppe | *Spokane* | 68 |
| Brits, The | *Longview* | 69 |
| Carnelian Rose Tea Company | *Vancouver* | 70 |
| Cheshire Cat Tea Shoppe | *Vancouver* | 71 |
| Christine's Tea Cottage | *Burlington* | 72 |
| Country Cottage Tea Parties | *Kirkland* | 73 |
| Elizabeth & Alexander Tea Room | *Bothell* | 74 |
| Enchanted Tea Garden | *Tacoma* | 75 |
| Everything Tea | *Snohomish* | 76 |
| Exhibitors Mall & Café | *Puyallup* | 77 |
| Fotheringham House | *Spokane* | 78 |
| Hattie's Restaurant | *Castle Rock* | 80 |
| Hattie's Tea Room | *Stanwood* | 81 |
| Ivy Tea Room | *College Place* | 82 |
| Just Pretend | *Port Townsend* | 83 |

# Tea Rooms Index - Washington
## Alphabetical Listing
*(City Listing on page 228)*

| | | |
|---|---|---|
| La Conner Flats - A Garden | *Mount Vernon* | 84 |
| La La Land Chocolates | *Port Gamble* | 85 |
| La Tea Da Teas at the Bradley House | *Cathlamet* | 86 |
| | | |
| Madison's Tea Room | *Marysville* | 87 |
| McGregor's Scottish Tea Rooms | *Tacoma* | 88 |
| Mr. Spots Chai House | *Seattle* | 89 |
| Mrs. Pennycooke's Tea Room | *Snohomish* | 90 |
| | | |
| Peach Tree Bakery & Tea Room | *Bothell* | 91 |
| Perennial Tea Room | *Seattle* | 92 |
| Petals Garden Café | *Sequim* | 93 |
| Piccadilly Circus | *Snohomish* | 94 |
| Pleasant Times Tea House | *Endicott* | 95 |
| Pomeroy Carriage House Tea Room | *Yacolt* | 96 |
| | | |
| Queen Mary Tea Room | *Seattle* | 98 |
| | | |
| Rose B&B and Tea Room | *Gig Harbor* | 99 |
| Rose Room at Whyel Museum | *Bellevue* | 100 |
| | | |
| Sadie's Tea Room | *Bellingham* | 101 |
| Sassy Tea House & Boutique | *Redmond* | 102 |
| Scottish Tea Shop Ltd. | *Seattle* | 103 |
| Secret Garden Tea Room | *Bellevue* | 104 |
| | | |
| Victorian Rose Tea Room | *Port Orchard* | 105 |
| Victorian Tea Connection | *Kennewick* | 106 |
| Victorian Tea Garden | *Richland* | 107 |
| Vintage Inn B&B and Tea Parlour | *Vancouver* | 108 |
| | | |
| Wild Sage Teas | *Port Townsend* | 109 |
| | | |
| Your Cup of Tea | | 110 |

# Tea Rooms Index - British Columbia
## Alphabetical Listing
(City Listing on page 231)

Applewood Tea Room                          *North Delta*        112

Bacchus Restaurant/Wedgewood Hotel  *Vancouver*        113
Blethering Place Tea Room                    *Victoria*           114
Butchart Gardens                            *Brentwood Bay*      115

Chocolate Cottage & Tea Garden          *Langley*            116
Clancy's Tea Cozy                           *White Rock*         117
Cottage Tea Room                            *Richmond*           118

Fairmont Empress Hotel Tea                   *Victoria*           119

Gatsby Mansion Inn                          *Victoria*           120

James Bay Tea Room                          *Victoria*           121
Jardin's                                    *Okahagan Falls*     122

London Heritage Farm                        *Richmond*           123

Roedde House Museum                         *Vancouver*          124

Secret Garden Tea Company                   *Vancouver*          125
Silk Road Tea Company                       *Victoria*           126
Sweet Revenge Patisserie                    *Vancouver*          127

White Heather Tea Room                      *Victoria*           128
Windsor House Tea Room                      *Victoria*           129

# Tea Rooms Index - Oregon
## City Listing
### (Alphabetical Listing on page 220)

### Albany
A La Fontaine . . . . . . . . . . . 16
Flinn's Tea Room . . . . . . . . . . 28
KJ's Tea House . . . . . . . . . . . 35

### Applegate
Eve's Garden Café & Tea Room . . . . . . 27

### Ashland
Ashland Springs Hotel . . . . . . . . . . 21

### Aurora
Butteville General Store . . . . . . . . . 23

### Bandon
Tea Cosy, The . . . . . . . . . . . . 53

### Bend
Tea Events . . . . . . . . . . . . 54
Tracy Hill Home & Garden . . . . . . . . 56

### Canby
Afternoon Tea by Stephanie . . . . . . . . 18

### Central Point
Once Upon a Time . . . . . . . . . . . 44

### Corvallis
Joyful Hearts . . . . . . . . . . . . 32
Sister Act Catering . . . . . . . . . . . 51

### Dallas
Althea's Tea Room . . . . . . . . . . . 20

# Tea Rooms Index - Oregon
## City Listing
### (Alphabetical Listing on page 220)

### Eugene
Campbell House Inn . . . . . . . . . . 24
Savoure . . . . . . . . . . . . . 49
Shelton-McMurphey-Johnson House . . . . . 50

### Florence
Mon Ami . . . . . . . . . . . . . . . 40

### Gresham
Rose's Tea Room . . . . . . . . . . . 47

### Hood River
Columbia Gorge Hotel . . . . . . . . . . 25

### Lake Oswego
Lady Di's Store & Tea Room . . . . . . . . 37

### Lebanon
Mrs. B's Special Teas . . . . . . . . . . 41

### McMinnville
Primrose Tea Room . . . . . . . . . . . 46

### Milwaukee
Blue Angel Heavenly Delectables . . . . . . 22

### Newport
Tea & Tomes, Ltd. . . . . . . . . . . . 52

# Tea Rooms Index - Oregon
## City Listing
### (Alphabetical Listing on page 220)

### Portland
Albertina's . . . . . . . . . . . . 19
Heathman Hotel Restaurant . . . . . . . . 30
In Good Taste . . . . . . . . . . . 31
Kashin-Tei Tea House . . . . . . . . . 34
Leach Botanical Garden . . . . . . . . 39
Tea Zone . . . . . . . . . . . . . 55
Wakai Tea Room . . . . . . . . . . 58

### Redmond
Wild Rose Tea Room, The . . . . . . . . 59

### Roseburg
Afternoon Delight . . . . . . . . . . 17

### Salem
Deepwood Estate . . . . . . . . . . 26
Julia's Tea Parlor . . . . . . . . . . 33
Nauna's Tea Room . . . . . . . . . . 42
Tudor Rose Tea Room . . . . . . . . . 57

### Sherwood
Lavender Tea House . . . . . . . . . . 38

### Silverton
Gordon House . . . . . . . . . . . 29
Oregon Tea Garden . . . . . . . . . . 45

### Springfield
Ruthie B's . . . . . . . . . . . . . 48

### St. Paul
Newell House Museum . . . . . . . . . 43

### Tillamook
La Tea Da Tea Room . . . . . . . . . 36

# Tea Rooms Index - Washington
## City Listing
### (Alphabetical Listing on page 222)

**Arlington**
Your Cup of Tea . . . . . . . . . . . 110

**Bellevue**
Rose Room at Whyel Museum . . . . . . . 100

**Bellingham**
Abbey Garden Tea Room . . . . . . . . . 63
Sadie's Tea Room . . . . . . . . . . . 101

**Bothel**
Elizabeth & Alexander English Tea Room . . . . 74
Peach Tree Bakery & Tea Room . . . . . . . 91

**Burlington**
Christine's Tea Cottage . . . . . . . . . 72

**Castle Rock**
Hattie's Restaurant . . . . . . . . . . . 80

**Cathlamet**
La Tea Da Teas at the Bradley House . . . . . 86

**College Place**
Ivy Tea Room . . . . . . . . . . . . . 82

**Coupeville**
Anna's Tea Room. . . . . . . . . . . . 66

**Endicott**
Pleasant Times . . . . . . . . . . . . 95

**Gig Harbor**
Rose B&B and Tea Room . . . . . . . . . 99

**Kennewick**
Victorian Tea Connection . . . . . . . . . 106

# Tea Rooms Index - Washington
## City Listing
### (Alphabetical Listing on page 222)

### Kirkland
Country Cottage Tea Parties . . . . . . . . 73

### Longview
Brits, The . . . . . . . . . . . . . 69

### Marysville
Attic Secrets Tea Room . . . . . . . . . . 67

### Mount Vernon
Althea's Tea Lounge. . . . . . . . . . . 65
La Conner Flats - a Garden. . . . . . . . . 84

### Port Gamble
La La Land Chocolates . . . . . . . . . . 85

### Port Orchard
Victorian Rose Tea Room . . . . . . . . . 105

### Port Townsend
Just Pretend . . . . . . . . . . . . . 83
Wild Sage Teas . . . . . . . . . . . 109

### Puyallup
Exhibitors Mall & Café . . . . . . . . . . 77

### Redmond
Sassy Tea House & Boutique . . . . . . . . 102
Victorian Tea Garden . . . . . . . . . . 107

# Tea Rooms Index - Washington
## City Listing
### (Alphabetical Listing on page 222)

### Seattle
Mr. Spots Chai House . . . . . . . . . . 89
Perennial Tea Room . . . . . . . . . . . 92
Queen Mary Tea Room . . . . . . . . . . 98
Scottish Tea Shop Ltd. . . . . . . . . . . 103

### Sequim
Petals Garden Café . . . . . . . . . . . . 93

### Snohomish
Everything Tea . . . . . . . . . . . . . 76
Mrs. Pennycooke's Tea Room . . . . . . . 90
Piccadilly Circus . . . . . . . . . . . . . 94

### Spokane
Brambleberry Cottage Tea Shoppe . . . . . . . 68
Fotheringham House . . . . . . . . . . . 78

### St. John
A Touch of Elegance . . . . . . . . . . . 62

### Stanwood
Hattie's Tea Room . . . . . . . . . . . . 81

### Tacoma
Enchanted Tea Garden . . . . . . . . . . 75
McGregor's Scottish Tea Room . . . . . . . 88

### Vancouver
Carnelian Rose Tea Company . . . . . . . . 70
Cheshire Cat Tea Shoppe . . . . . . . . . 71
Vintage Inn & Tea Parlor . . . . . . . . . 108

### Yacolt
Pomeroy Carriage House Tea Room . . . . . . . 96

# Tea Rooms Index - British Columbia

## City Listing
### (Alphabetical Listing on page 224)

### Brentwood Bay
Butchart Gardens . . . . . . . . . 115

### Langley
Chocolate Cottage . . . . . . . . . 116

### North Delta
Applewood Tea Room . . . . . . . . 112

### Richmond
Cottage Tea Room . . . . . . . . . 118
London Heritage Farm . . . . . . . . 123

### Vancouver
Bacchus Restaurant / Wedgewood Hotel . . . . 113
Roedde House Museum . . . . . . . 124
Secret Garden Tea Company . . . . . . 125
Sweet Revenge Patisserie . . . . . . . 127

### Victoria
Blethering Place Tea Room. . . . . . . . 114
Fairmont Empress Hotel Tea . . . . . . . 119
Gatsby Mansion Inn . . . . . . . . . 120
James Bay Tea Room . . . . . . . . 121
Silk Road Aromatherapy & Tea Company . . . . 126
White Heather Tea Room . . . . . . . 128
Windsor House Tea Room . . . . . . . 129

### White Rock
Clancy's Tea Cozy . . . . . . . . . 117

I believe that everyone who visits tea rooms and craft stores is familiar with the *Country Register*. It is usually set in a prominent place near the entrance, to insure that no one leaves without a copy. It works for us, and we look forward to each issue, anxious to see if any new tea rooms are listed

Barbara Floyd, the founder and publisher of the newspaper, is an entrepreneur at heart. When her children were young, she started an arts and crafts fundraiser for their school. When the school phased out that event, Barbara started one of the first "home" arts and crafts shows. It eventually became a gift shop close to her home. Along with her daughter, Barbra-Jean, she also created the first tea room and gift shop in Arizona. Under new ownership, "Gooseberries" is still operating in Phoenix, Arizona.

Needing an affordable means of advertising, Barbara started the *Arizona Country Register* in 1988. The paper has helped bond gift shop and tea room owners, crafters, quilters and customers together state wide. Eventually, people asked to start *Country Regis-*  *ters* in their own states and a licensing agreement was formed. There are now over 40 *Country Registers* in the United States and Canada. When Traveling, we have found the *Country Registe*r to be a wonderful resource for finding Tea Rooms. We also enjoy all of the tea related articles.

Thanks, Barbara, for your promotion of tea!

# About

# TeaTimeAdventures.Com

*Teatimeadventures.com* is your link to current information about the Tea Rooms listed in this guide and beyond. It will keep you posted on new tea purveyors as well as seasonal or permanent closures. When traveling you can preview the best tea offerings for your destination.

This web site provides a list of upcoming tea events, updated news, current happenings, a newsletter, recipes and much more. Please visit and enjoy this resource designed with tea lovers in mind and use our comments page to let us know what else may be of interest to you.

*teatimeadventures.com*

# Be a TEA ROOM Spotter

When you're out-n-about and discover a new tea spot, please let us know. Many of our best new "finds" come from tea spotters like you. *(Thank You for Sharing)*

## How to Report a New Tea Room

You can email the information to us at: *(demontigny@proaxis.com)* or use our web site comments page *(teatimeadventures.com)* or if you prefer to mail it in, sent the information requested below with the Tea Rooms business card, and a flyer if possible to:

Tea Rooms Northwest Staff
2397 NW Kings Blvd. # 148
Corvallis, Oregon 97330

Tea Room Name:_____

Contact Person:_____

Address:_____

City:_____

State/Province/Zip:_____

Phone:_____

Referred by:_____

Address:_____

City:_____

State/Province/Zip:_____

# *Is Journaling for You?*

Journaling is a wonderful lasting keepsake of your time spent with family and friends enjoying a tea time experience. Keeping a journal can nurture your sentimental side and feed the desire to capture special moments in your life.

If you are smitten by the tea experience as we are, then journaling is for you. Our mission is to promote your tea room experience as much as possible! If you have "Tea Room" memories you would like to save, then journaling is for you.

The TEA TIME JOURNAL is a unique journal and measures 8 ½" x 5 ½". The 80 page book features space to journal 30 tea room visits. You can record your observations on the menus, presentations, service, and more. The TEATIME JOURNAL includes a tea glossary, trivia, tea facts, our favorite scone recipe, tea quiz, and plenty of room for your thoughts and inspirations. The TEA TIME JOURNAL is the perfect gift for all tea lovers.

For ordering information see next page or visit our internet site at *teatimeadventures.com* and click on "journaling".

# A Tea Time Journal
### is the perfect gift for
### tea lovers everywhere

To order copies of the
TEA TIME JOURNAL for yourself
or fellow tea lover, please
provide us with the information
below or make a photocopy of this page.
Send your order along with a
check or money order
in the amount of $11.95 USD
($9.95 + $2.00 S&H US only)
(for forging shipments, please inquire)

## J&S Publishing
2397 N.W. Kings Blvd. # 148
Corvallis, Oregon 97330 USA

If you prefer to pay by credit card,
you may do so on the web at:
*www.paypal.com*

Name: _____

Address: _____

City: _____

State/Providence/Zip: _____

*You may also contact at:*
*demontigny@proaxis.com*

# New Tea Room Discoveries

# New Tea Room Discoveries